Date Due

DEC 16 MAY 18		
JAN 4 NOV 17 1988		
JAN 20		
MAR 2		
APR 2		
APR 13		
26		
MAY 27		
FEB 18		
JAN 3		
JAN 23		
MAY 8		
MAY 22		
OCT 6		
JAN 11		
FEB 24		
ℬ	PRINTED IN U. S. A.	

Inventive Wizard

GEORGE WESTINGHOUSE

Born: October 6, 1846

Died: March 12, 1914

Beginning with the invention of a crude cutting machine when he was twelve, Westinghouse spent all his life inventing machines and equipment. Among his most important inventions are air brakes and signal devices which revolutionized the railroad industry and the shock absorber for automobiles. His work on transmitting electricity at low cost brought power and light to millions of people. The story of the dramatic battles George Westinghouse fought to bring his many discoveries into practical use is one of the most important chapters of our Industrial Age.

Inventive Wizard

GEORGE WESTINGHOUSE

by I. E. Levine

 JULIAN MESSNER, INC.
NEW YORK

Published by Julian Messner, Inc.
8 West 40 Street, New York 18

Published simultaneously in Canada
by The Copp Clark Publishing Co. Limited

© Copyright 1962 by I. E. Levine

Third Printing, 1963

Printed in the United States of America
Library of Congress Catalog Card No. 62-10192

This book is for my daughter Carol

Contents

Inventive Wizard

GEORGE WESTINGHOUSE

1

Home Is the Sailor

A DISMAL GRAY MIST HUNG OVER NEW YORK CITY LIKE AN oppressive blanket on the morning of July 15, 1865. Along the cobblestoned streets crowds of bystanders gathered in silence to watch the long lines of soldiers in their faded blue uniforms marching home from war.

The Civil War was over. Two months before, the angry roar of the cannon had been heard for the last time. Now the men who had fought and bled were coming home at last—to the farms and factories and families they had left behind. As they tramped along the steaming streets of the great city there were no cheers or shouts of triumph—only a grim silent sadness haunted by the memories of bloody battle-fields and long lines of white crosses marking the graves of those who would not return.

On a curbstone an old man wearing a black armband watched the columns of blue-clad soldiers through moist eyes. He brushed away a tear and mumbled something to no one in particular. The words were drowned in the cadence of marching feet.

A tall young man in a naval uniform who was watching the parade observed the old man for a moment. Finally he spoke up. "Is anything wrong, sir?"

"No, lad," was the reply. "I only remarked they are so young and yet their eyes are old from having seen death and suffering."

The youthful sailor remained silent. The old man studied him carefully. "Why, you are only a boy yourself," he said. The young man self-consciously began to stroke the dark blond mustache and beard he had cultivated so zealously to hide his youth and said in a mildly offended voice, "I am nineteen, sir!"

"Nineteen," the old man repeated and broke into a gentle smile. "I didn't mean to insult you, lad. You see, my son would have been nineteen last month. He was killed at Nashville."

The young man noted the black band on the old man's arm. "I'm sorry, sir," he said softly. Then, as if to console him, he added, "My older brother Albert was killed last winter, too. He was a lieutenant with the Second New York Veteran Volunteer Cavalry. He was shot down while leading a charge at McLeod's Mills in Louisiana."

"I recall reading the newspaper account of the engagement," the old man said. "It was a bloody affair. And you—have you seen battle, too?"

The youth shook his head. "Not really. I've been stationed with the Potomac Flotilla as a third assistant engineer, first aboard the *Muscoota* and then on the *Stars and Stripes*. Before that I was with the Sixteenth New York Volunteer Cavalry when I asked to be transferred to the Navy. Except for patrol action, I have not seen battle."

"Are you from the city, lad?" the old man inquired.

"No, sir, from Schenectady. I was let out of the service two days ago and arrived in New York this morning. Now I am waiting for a train to take me home. It leaves this afternoon."

The old man looked up at the tall young man and noted that he had strong, regular features and innocent blue eyes. "You remind me of my son. I like you. What is your name?"

"George Westinghouse, sir."

"Well, I'm pleased to meet you, George Westinghouse. I wish you the best of luck. I shall remember your name, and perhaps one day I will hear great things about you."

The old man left then and was swallowed up in the crowd.

Later, when George Westinghouse boarded his train he thought of his encounter with the old bystander and felt strangely moved. War had left its mark on everyone, he thought. He knew what it meant to lose someone you love; he had seen the deep tragedy in his mother's eyes when he came home on furlough soon after his brother Albert's death.

Of the five boys and three girls in the large Westinghouse family, Albert unquestionably had been the parents' favorite. Placid and soft-spoken, he had an instinct for doing the right thing at the right time and was almost never in trouble. Mrs. Westinghouse often said, "Albert is a perfect son. Since the day he was born he hasn't given me a moment's worry."

George was convinced that the blow to his parents was deeper than if he or one of his other brothers had fallen in battle. He could not help feeling vague stirrings of guilt at having escaped from the war unscarred. He recalled that of all the children he had given his parents the most anguish during the growing-up years.

Perhaps there was some truth in the saying, "The good die young." If it were not so, how could anyone explain poor Albert's untimely death and his own remarkable good fortune in having emerged without a scratch?

These were some of the thoughts that haunted nineteen-year-old George Westinghouse as the train engine churned up its head of steam and puffed noisily out of the station. He stared through the grimy window, intent on enjoying the magnificent scenery. Soon majestic palisades appeared in the west as they chugged up the east bank of the beautiful Hudson River. The sun had broken through and driven away the morning's mist. Now its reflection glistened from the glassy surface of the water as if from a mirror. The scene was almost unreal, and it cast a hypnotic spell on the young veteran.

It reminded him of his own boyhood days amid the lush rolling hills and silver streams of upper New York State.

His earliest memories were of playing in the back yard of the large white rambling frame house in Central Bridge. It was the house in which he was born. Until he was six the house and the fields beyond were his entire world.

Central Bridge, a small village in New York's beautiful Schoharie Valley, was situated at the juncture of the Schoharie River and Cobleskill Creek. Here, on October 6, 1846, George Westinghouse, Jr., had arrived in the world and announced immediately via a sturdy pair of lungs that he was not a child to be ignored.

Nevertheless, with three boys and three girls already in the family, George's arrival was accepted without panic by his parents, George Westinghouse, Sr., and Emmeline Vedder Westinghouse. He had been named after his father at his mother's insistence.

"He looks like you, George," she told her husband softly. "He's the only one of the children who doesn't take after my side of the family. He's big-boned, like you, and he has that same determined look in his eye."

George Westinghouse, a huge man well over six feet, grinned sheepishly. Indeed, he *was* a determined man. Of German descent, he had been born and reared in Vermont. There he had inherited the self-reliance and deep sense of purpose of two generations of New England forebears. He had met Emmeline Vedder, a comely, attractive girl of Dutch-English stock, in North Pownal, Vermont, and they fell in love immediately.

Soon after their marriage in 1831 George, Sr., and his bride pulled up stakes, piled their meager belongings on the back of a horse-drawn wagon and made the long trek to the Ohio frontier which was rumored to be a land of golden opportunity. But these stories of the fortunes to be made in the newly opened west proved to be exaggerations. The land was rocky and the climate disagreed with Emmeline, so five years later they decided to return east.

Although born and bred a farmer, George discovered during the stay in Ohio that he had a natural talent for

working with tools and machinery. With infinite patience
and determination he taught himself to become a skilled
carpenter and general mechanic. By the time they returned
from Ohio in 1836 the ambitious self-trained young husband
was ready to give up farming and set himself up in business.

On the trip back they paused in Central Bridge, a quaint
village in a peaceful, mossy valley thirty-six miles west of
Albany, New York. George Westinghouse looked the town
over carefully. He noted it was located in a region of fertile,
well-tilled farms. There was also a sprinkling of schools,
churches and even some newly built factories.

Finally, he stuck out a stubborn, granite jaw, turned to
his wife and said, "Emmeline, this is a good place to live
and to raise a family. Here is where we will settle." His
wife, bone-weary after the hard trip from Ohio, nodded
assent.

They took an option on a tract of land containing some
small buildings and converted one of them into a machine
shop. Since it was at the very juncture of Cobleskill Creek
and the Schoharie River, water power was available at
George's doorstep. Within a few months he managed to develop a thriving business repairing machinery for the nearby
mills. Then he branched out and began to manufacture
threshing machines, seedscrapers and other agricultural appliances for the farmers in the region.

As the business grew, the Westinghouse family grew, too.
By the time George was born in 1846 the firm of G. Westinghouse & Co. was known far beyond the valley. The Westinghouses, with their three sons and three daughters, were
among the leading families of Central Bridge.

With the birth of George, Jr., however, the family's quiet
well-ordered life underwent a transformation. The other six
children were quiet, well-behaved youngsters, especially Albert, who by his example seemed to exercise a wholesome
influence on his brothers and sisters.

But George, Jr., was not like the others. Stubborn, high-
spirited and temperamental from the first, he was not ame-

nable to the usual parental discipline. When he wanted
something, he demanded it, and when it was refused, he had
a tantrum. He shouted and screamed and beat his head
against the ground until it was bloody.

By the time little George was ready for school, Mr. and
Mrs. Westinghouse were at their wits' end. "I don't know
how to handle the boy," the mother told her husband de-
spairingly. "We can't forever give in to him. Yet I don't
know how to put up with his displays of temper when I say
no. If he does the same thing in school, the schoolmaster
will send him home."

To the elder George, coping with his son was a formidable
challenge. For one thing there was now a new baby named
Herman, who, being the youngest, demanded a good deal
of his mother's time. Moreover, in young George the father
could see mirrored his own personality. Physically, the boy
was a chip off the old block. He seemed to be shooting up
like a sprout and was already taller than two of his older
brothers. His facial features and expressions resembled his
father's to an uncanny degree, but most significant, he had
inherited his father's stubborn sense of pride and determination. He had George senior's driving force and independent
spirit.

Deep down, Mr. Westinghouse knew he and his son were
alike. So out of some half-hidden recognition and acceptance
of himself, he sympathized with the boy and found it hard
to be angry with him. Yet there were times when he could
not understand little George at all. He tried to reason with
him, but sometimes it had little effect.

"Do you want others to think you're disrespectful to your
elders?" he asked the lad soberly. "In this world you must
live with other people. You cannot always have your own
way. You must learn to accept it with good grace when your
mother or I say no to you, just as your brothers and sisters do."

On rare occasions George, Jr., seemed to accept this argument. But just as his father was about to congratulate him-

self on having made some headway, the youngster would slip
back to his old unmanageable behavior. He would demand
a toy or cookie, and when his mother refused, he would give
way to agonized tears and ear-piercing shrieks.

Finally, Mr. Westinghouse could stand it no longer. He
had always prided himself on his ability to control his children through the use of reason rather than corporal punishment. With the other children it took no more than a mean-
ingful glance or a single word softly spoken to make them
realize the error of their ways. Except on one or two rare
occasions he had never raised a finger against them. With
young George, more stringent measures seemed to be called
for.

One day, the boy got into an argument with a neighbor's
small son. Although they were the same age, George was a
head taller and pounds heavier. The argument progressed,
until the smaller boy pointed at George and shouted, "I
don't want to fight with you because you're crazy. You have
fits. My mother and father say so."

Without fully realizing the nature of the insult George
sensed that it was a serious one. So he charged into the other
boy and pummeled him to the ground. By the time Albert,
who had seen the scuffle from a distance, came over and
separated them, George had hit the other boy in the eye.

For Mr. Westinghouse, who was given a full account of
the fight by the victim's parents, it was the straw that broke
the camel's back.

"George, why did you beat that boy?" he demanded.

"He said I was crazy."

"Is that the only reason?"

"Yes," George replied. He bit his lip in frustration, for
try as he might he knew he could not explain to his father
the deep mortification he had felt at the insult.

The father stared down angrily at his son. "You are bigger
than that boy, and heavier. You blackened his eye. If you
had not been stopped by Albert you might have injured him
seriously. Do you think I can overlook the matter, George?"

The boy looked up meekly. "No, Father."

"Then come to the stable with me!"

Mr. Westinghouse left the house and strode purposefully along the stone-covered path to the sprawling stable, followed by his small son. At that moment the lad felt a curious mixture of stubborn pride and fear of physical punishment.

In the stable the father picked up an ancient switch and ordered young George to bend over. He obeyed dutifully.

Whack!

The switch came down smartly. The boy cried out, though more in fear than pain. He heard his father grumble in annoyance and looked up. The switch had broken in two.

Mr. Westinghouse studied the broken switch uncertainly. Then his son spoke up tearfully and pointed a chubby finger at a length of leather harness hanging on the wall. "You can use that, Father. It's stronger and won't break."

The man looked at his small son for a long moment, not knowing whether to laugh or cry. Then he said slowly, as if finding it difficult to speak, "No, son. There will be no more whipping this day."

By the time George entered school the infantile outbursts of temper had disappeared. He was still quick to anger, however, and other youngsters, including his brothers and sisters, did not hesitate to exploit his sensitivity by teasing him. He soon became a sort of scapegoat among the neighborhood children. Often, when they made fun of him, he bridled and raised his small fists pugnaciously. After numerous fights, many of which resulted in beatings at the hands of the older boys, he learned an important lesson: if he stayed away from the other children, they could not taunt him.

From that moment on young George Westinghouse began to spend more and more of his time in a tiny circumscribed world of his own. Alone, he explored the fields and streams near Central Bridge, and on a balmy spring afternoon he loved nothing better than to lie down under a large shade tree and stare up at the blue sky and marvel at the astonish-

ing tricks Nature had up her sleeve. He wondered what made
it possible for birds to fly effortlessly, and about the strange
cycle of growth that enabled a tiny seed planted in the rich
black earth to become a stalk of tall golden grain. How did
these things happen? he asked himself. Perhaps someday
when he grew older he would learn the answers.

In school George was an apathetic pupil except for mathematics and free-hand drawing, in which he excelled. His
teachers complained to his parents constantly.

"It isn't as if George is incapable of learning," they said
ruefully. "He is. In fact, he is one of the most intelligent
children in the school. Except for mathematics and art work
he simply doesn't apply himself to the other subjects."

About this time the boy discovered the wonders of his
father's machine shop. This was surprising considering that
none of his three older brothers had any interest in mechanical work. Jay, the oldest, had a strong aptitude for business
management. John, next in age, was interested in religion
and social problems. Albert, who loved good literature and
was an ingenious debater, seemed destined for a career at
the bar. And Baby Herman, of course, was much too young
to show a serious talent for anything but children's games.

George had visited his father's shop even as a toddler and
had been entranced by the sight of the machinery. Now, as
he learned how the tools and complex mechanisms were
used, he was delighted by the many operations a skilled
worker could perform with them. He gave up walking in the
fields and studying the sky in favor of visiting the shop
where the din of heavy machinery was music to his ears and
he could drink in the smell of fresh grease and hot iron.

He pleaded with his father to teach him to use tools, and
finally Mr. Westinghouse said yes. He assigned some of the
experienced workers to show his son the safe and proper
way to handle equipment. George learned quickly. Within
a few months he knew how to read simple blueprints and
could set up a lathe to perform the more elementary operations.

One of the employees, a good-natured foreman named Rathbone, admired the boy's natural aptitude for mechanics and rigged up a small den in the loft of the building for use as an amateur workshop. Soon the boy was spending most of his afternoons tinkering away to his heart's content on a variety of simple devices, such as miniature water wheels and tiny steam engines.

Before long, Mr. Westinghouse discovered that his son's daily visits to the machine shop were becoming a full-time pursuit. He reluctantly admitted to himself that he had made a serious error in granting this privilege. George had been an apathetic student before, but now he was almost failing in school. On several occasions, when the elder Westinghouse had to go out of town on business, he returned to find that the boy had missed classes in order to spend time in the little workroom.

His worries were multiplied by the realization that his son did not show a healthy interest in playing with other children. He confided to his wife Emmeline that something must be done. She agreed. But what?

"I'll order him not to come to the shop!" he fumed. "His place is in the classroom, else he'll never amount to anything."

"But won't that only encourage him to do secretly what we forbid him to do openly?" Mrs. Westinghouse observed with quiet sagaciousness.

Her husband scratched his chin thoughtfully. She was right. Still, something had to be done.

"Why can't we let him spend time in the shop but limit it to one or two hours daily," Mrs. Westinghouse continued. "What's more, he'll have to earn the privilege by making passing grades in his subjects."

George, Sr., agreed to the plan, and it worked.

Fearful that the privilege of working in the shop would be taken away, the boy began to devote a minimum of effort to school. His marks improved although he was still hostile to such subjects as penmanship, spelling and grammar.

The momentary problem was solved, but George Westinghouse, Sr., was not rid of a gnawing sense of uneasiness. Secretly, he was flattered that at least one of his sons had inherited his dexterity with tools and his love of machinery. But he worried, too, that George might decide to become an ordinary shop mechanic.

It wasn't that he was a snob. After all, he was a mechanic himself, and a good one, proud of his skill and success in building a prosperous business. No, he had nothing to be ashamed of. But like many successful men who depended on their hands to earn a livelihood, it had been his ambition for his sons to become professional men. He had dreamed fine dreams of sending the boys to college so they could become doctors or lawyers or ministers. In George's case he saw the nullification of these dreams.

By 1856, when George was ten, G. Westinghouse & Co. was doing so well its owner decided a major expansion was in order. He entered into a partnership agreement with two brothers named Clute and agreed to move the factory to Schenectady where the cost of obtaining materials was cheaper and transportation more convenient.

The firm bought a building formerly used as a cement mill on the south bank of the Erie Canal and turned it into a factory. At the same time, the Westinghouse family moved from Central Bridge into a large handsome brick house in the city.

It had been Mr. Westinghouse's hope that the new surroundings would change his unusual ten-year-old son whose sole pleasure stemmed from tinkering with machines and tools. But this hope was soon dashed. The new factory with its newer, up-to-date machinery only whetted George's appetite.

However, the move to Schenectady did have one beneficial effect. It improved the boy's attitude toward his studies. In the city he was placed in the charge of a teacher who finally understood him. From the moment George entered her classroom, Alice Gilbert knew instinctively that he was a boy with unusual gifts and must be handled in an unusual way.

To George's amazement she actually encouraged him to develop his mechanical interests! This was a complete reversal of his treatment in the Central Bridge school where he had been scolded and criticized by his teachers for the same thing.

"If you are wise you will explore everything that interests you," Miss Gilbert told him. "That is the only way to open doors to a rich, full life."

Slowly, step by step, she also led him into exploring the subjects he had always disliked and shied away from.

"What is it you wish to be, George? A great scientist? A statesman? A famous general?" she inquired patiently. "To be good at anything you must also develop a broad understanding of the world you live in. You must explore different areas of human knowledge before you dismiss them as unimportant. You will be surprised at how interesting you will find things if only you give yourself half a chance. Do you understand, George?"

He nodded uncertainly, but as the months passed he found that Miss Gilbert had an amazing gift for making even dull subjects come alive. She had read a great deal and the facts she gave about history and literature—yes, even grammar—were interesting and vital.

George soon discovered he had a gift for writing. She encouraged him to write his composition assignments about machinery and shopwork and the other subjects that interested him. When he wrote about science or mechanics he found he could do so simply and lucidly, although in the past he had always loathed writing. Now he began to enjoy the sense of accomplishment it gave him.

George Westinghouse, Sr., was confused by what was taking place. All along he had been worried about his son's single-track interest in mechanics, and now he discovered that the teacher had actually been encouraging the boy! He and his wife decided to visit the school and have a long talk with Miss Gilbert. They told her frankly that they were disturbed at the turn of events.

"George is an unusual boy, Mr. Westinghouse," she reassured them. "He's sensitive and strong-spirited. Many gifted children are like that. We must lead them to explore all the avenues they can, in the hope that sooner or later they will find their proper place. If George likes tools and machines, it is a good thing to encourage him in it. At the same time, we must see that he does not neglect other areas of his education."

She then described the progress she was making in kindling George's interest in his schoolwork.

"Even so, Miss Gilbert, don't you feel he's too young to spend as much time as he does in my shop?" Mr. Westinghouse wanted to know. "The way he's going, I fear he'll wind up as an ordinary mechanic. Mrs. Westinghouse and I had higher hopes for our youngsters."

Miss Gilbert smiled and said, "Too often parents try to force their children into a preconceived mold. George, of course, is too strong-willed for that. Regardless of your ambitions for him, if he decides to become a mechanic there is little you can do to turn him from it. Nor will anyone be able to force him to turn his hand to a career he doesn't like. Personally, I'm convinced that the lad is too bright and volatile to be satisfied with a career as a simple mechanical worker."

The talk with Miss Gilbert was reassuring. When the Westinghouses left the school that afternoon George, Sr., had reached a firm decision.

2

Youthful Patriot

"GEORGE!"

"Yes, Father?"

"Come here. I want to talk to you."

The boy approached warily. What had he done now? Was he in serious trouble? He searched his father's face for a clue, but the stolid expression told him nothing.

"George," Mr. Westinghouse began quietly, "I have a proposition for you. Are you interested in a job in the machine shop?"

The youngster was immediately on his guard. The proposal had come as a complete surprise. For months his father had criticized him for spending too much time in the shop. Now he was being asked to work there!

"Do you mean for wages, Father?" he ventured cautiously.

Mr. Westinghouse smiled. "Yes, lad. For wages. It's now June. Soon school will be out. If you're agreeable, I'll take you on as an apprentice mechanic for the summer vacation."

George wanted to jump with joy, but he held himself in check and tried to appear businesslike. "What wage will I be paid, sir?"

His father suppressed a grin and cleared his throat. "Well, I was thinking two dollars a week would be fair pay for a beginning apprentice."

George wrinkled his eyebrows thoughtfully as he had

often seen his father do when discussing business matters. Finally he nodded. "Two dollars a week will be fair, Father."

"Good. Then it's settled. But remember, lad, you will be an employee—not the owner's son. You will have to earn your wage and expect to be treated like any other apprentice. You will work a full day every day, six days a week, and you will take your orders from the foreman. Is that understood?"

The boy nodded vigorously, trying hard to conceal his glee.

Emmeline Westinghouse was not convinced of the wisdom of the plan. "After all the child is only twelve," she told her husband. "To have him work in the shop for nine or ten hours a day throughout the hot summer—well, it just doesn't seem right, no matter what it is you are trying to prove."

"Nonsense, Emmeline dear, George is a big strapping lad," Mr. Westinghouse argued. "Hard work will do him good. Besides, if his teacher is right when she says he's too stubborn to be discouraged, let him see for himself what it means to work in a factory for wages. That, if nothing else, will convince him the life of an ordinary mechanic is not what he imagines it to be. It's one thing to tinker around with his little toys when he feels like it and quite another to have to do what he is told to do, whether he likes it or not. Why it may make a man of him. He'll learn self-discipline, something we seem to have taught him precious little of."

Reluctantly, Mrs. Westinghouse agreed to her husband's plan.

George's first day on the job was not at all what he had expected. His father had warned him he would be treated like any other apprentice, but in his boyish enthusiasm he had not realized what this meant. Naturally he had assumed he would be assigned to some interesting work on the lathe or one of the new planers that had just recently arrived from England. Instead, he was ordered to sweep up the metal shavings that littered the machine-shop floor.

He protested, but one of the senior mechanics cut him short.

"We'll have no back talk from an apprentice," the man growled, trying hard to keep from laughing. "Do as you're told, boy!"

George did as he was told, but he felt humiliated. After all, these were the same men to whom he had grown attached in the past months. During his visits to the shop they had taught him how to use the tools and machinery. On occasion they had even shared their lunches with him. Now they were different; they acted gruff and businesslike. Why had they changed?

During the lunch period he complained to his father that he was getting all the dirty jobs to do. Mr. Westinghouse sympathized but would not budge an inch to intervene.

"An apprentice is the lowest ranking employee in the shop," he explained solemnly. "He's expected to do all the menial tasks. If it will make you feel better, bear in mind that every one of these men had to go through an apprenticeship, too."

George bit his lip but said no more about it. All afternoon he silently swept the floor. It was a never-ending job. As soon as one end of the shop was clean the other was covered with shavings and metal dust, but George continued to work diligently. At the end of the day he swept up for the last time until the entire floor was spotless. Then he moved the heavy buckets of shavings and scrap metal outside where they would be picked up the next morning by the wagon from the forging company. When he got home his bones ached from the long day's work, but he did not complain.

For the rest of the week his only task was to sweep the floor. The following Monday, however, he was assigned to clean up the equipment, too. It was a grimy business. The machines were usually drenched with grease and oil, and before he left for the day he had to scrub them with stiff brushes and rags until the steel gleamed. When he finished, his face and hands were black and it took him half an hour to wash away the grease so he would look presentable at the dinner table. But still he did not complain.

His father, who frankly had expected him to quit after the second or third day, was amazed that he was sticking it out. Mr. Westinghouse went so far as to hint that if George asked him to, he would even consider modifying their original agreement.

"It's turning out to be a hot summer, lad," his father observed at dinner one evening. "Would you like to work only in the mornings so you'll have the afternoons free for swimming?"

"No, Father," replied George. "I agreed to work full time, and I mean to do it."

Mr. Westinghouse shrugged and reached for a slice of freshly baked bread; his wife said nothing, but her lips grew taut. The other Westinghouse children stared at their brother as if he were a lunatic.

In the shop however the men gained a wholesome respect for the stubborn twelve-year-old. It was true they had always been fond of their employer's son who asked so many questions and seemed to have a genuine love for the complicated machines under their command. Now they couldn't help admiring his determination as well.

He had taken the initial hazing like a man, so they began to ease up in their treatment of him. The foreman assigned him as a helper to the lathe mechanics. He already knew much about lathe work and found it more interesting than being a "clean-up" man. Nevertheless, having to perform the same operations over and over struck him as dull and tedious.

One steaming Saturday at the end of July the temperature was ninety-five. The shop was a giant furnace. The men stripped to their waists, but the sweat continued to pour off their faces and backs. By mid-morning, work had become virtually impossible.

Mr. Westinghouse stepped out of the cubbyhole that served him as an office and got the men's attention. "After lunch, we will close for the rest of the day," he announced. "The time off will be on the company. Everyone will receive his regular wage."

The men cheered. They went back to their machines with renewed vigor. Someone slapped George on the back enthusiastically. "Your father is a good man to work for, boy," he grinned. "I'll fight the man who'll tell me different."

George returned to his lathe whistling happily. The water in the creek down by the canal would be clean and cool, he thought as he shivered with pleasure in anticipation of the refreshing swim he would have there in the afternoon.

However, just before lunch his father summoned him into the office. "George, I have bad news for you," he said. "We've just received a rush order for two threshers. They must be finished by the end of next week. It's an important order, and it means we must begin cutting a dozen lengths of iron pipe so the men can start constructing the machines first thing Monday morning."

For a moment the full meaning of his father's words did not sink in. "I'm glad our company got the order," he replied. "Is that all, Father?"

Mr. Westinghouse studied his son for a moment. "I don't think you understand. We must begin cutting the pipes to length *this afternoon*. I'm assigning you to that job."

The boy's face fell. "Me? Why me, Father? You've given everyone the afternoon off! I had planned to go swimming."

Mr. Westinghouse was uncomfortable. Clearly he did not relish the idea of going back on his word to his son. "I regret having to disappoint you, George, I really do, but the order came in after I made the announcement to the men. The only fair decision was to give the job to the lowest ranking employee. That's you."

"But it isn't fair," the boy protested, close to tears. "I've worked hard and tried to earn my wage."

"I know that, son," his father replied firmly but unhappily. "Nevertheless it was the fairest solution I could find, so I'm afraid you'll have to stay and work."

There was no point in arguing further. George left the office with tears of anger welling in his eyes.

By the end of the lunch hour the entire shop knew what had happened. They patted the boy on the shoulder sympathetically. "Too bad, son. But that's the way it is when you work for a wage."

After lunch the men cleaned up their tools and machines and left. The shop was empty now and quiet except for the chirping of a swallow outside the window.

George was full of self-pity. It was unfair of his father, he decided. Indeed it was unfair for anyone to have to work on a Saturday afternoon. Inspired by his feeling of martyrdom, he made a sudden resolve. "If ever I own my own shop," he declared half aloud, "I will give the men *every* Saturday afternoon off, as well as Sunday. And I'll pay them their full wages!"

Spiritually strengthened by his own generosity, he began to examine the job that had to be done. He surveyed the lengths of pipe stacked neatly in their wooden rack, but the discouraging sight renewed his feeling of despair. Cutting them to proper lengths would be a grueling job. Each piece had to be sawed by hand. He estimated that if he worked steadily all afternoon he might be able to finish four or five pieces by nightfall. The rest would have to be cut Monday, but at least it would give the men enough pipe to begin construction of the threshing machines.

He began to drag a long piece of pipe out of the rack to mount it on the sawhorses. Suddenly he stopped as his eye fell on the huge steam engine used to power the metal-working machines. An inspiration dawned! Why cut the pipes by hand at all? Why couldn't he clamp the saw to one of the lathes and do the job with the help of steam power? By pressing the blade of the saw against the pipe while the pipe rotated in the lathe he could cut through the metal as easily as a knife slices cheese!

In the flush of discovery George forgot the stifling heat and his feelings of self-pity and resentment. The onerous

chore had now become a challenge—a challenge he would
meet even if it meant working all night!

Fortunately the steam engine was still fired up. Working
swiftly, George used clamps to mount a small steel handsaw
on the slide rest of one of the large lathes. Normally the
slide rest was used to hold the cutting tools for shaping the
turning metal, but with the saw clamped in place it was
now converted into a primitive pipe-cutting tool.

He marked off one of the lengths of pipe for proper size,
placed it in the lathe, turned on the power. The machine
started up with a rumble. The pipe was soon rotating at
high speed. Carefully, he moved the slide rest until the saw
blade bit into the spinning pipe. There was an ear-splitting
whine as the steel teeth sliced through the iron. In a matter
of seconds, the pipe was cut! It was wonderful how effortlessly the device worked. In moments, he had completed a
job which, if done in the accepted way, would have taken
twenty minutes or a half hour of the hardest physical labor.

George examined the cut pipe carefully. It was a far better
job than could have been done by a skilled mechanic sawing
by hand. Delighted with his success, he proceeded to cut the
rest of the pipe. In less than an hour the entire job was done.
He stacked the twelve pieces of pipe, sawed to required size,
in a bin and stepped back to consider his achievement. At
that moment twelve-year-old George Westinghouse became
fully aware for the first time in his life that through machines
the human race had found the means to change its destiny.

Sobered somewhat by the enormity of this realization,
he locked the door of the shop and strolled reflectively
down the street toward the creek. In a secluded spot, he
threw off his clothes and plunged naked into the clear, cool
water.

A half hour later, feeling cleansed and refreshed, he went
home. Mr. Westinghouse, catnapping in the hammock, heard
him coming up the walk and sat up.

"What are you doing home, George? You had a job to do."

"Yes, Father. I did it."

Mr. Westinghouse took out his gold pocket watch and stared at it incredulously. "Why it's only three-thirty. What's the matter with you, boy?"

"I know, sir. The pipes are cut to size."

His father glared angrily. "That's a poor joke, George, and I don't appreciate it. Why it would have taken two men all afternoon to have cut those pipes."

"No, Father, I cut them all," he said with a smug grin.

Mr. Westinghouse climbed out of the hammock. "Very well," he said coldly. "We'll get to the bottom of this right now. You'll return to the shop with me."

The father walked swiftly, his long legs moving like pistons. George almost had to run to keep up with him. When they got to the shop, the boy unlocked the door and pointed to the bin. His father stared at the neatly stacked pipes in amazement. Only then did George explain how he had done it. Mr. Westinghouse was speechless. On the way home he walked slowly, thoughtfully, with the boy beside him. Finally, he threw an arm around the youngster's shoulder and said with quiet pride, "George, though you're my own flesh and blood I don't think I'll ever quite know what to make of you."

When school resumed in the fall a full-time job was out of the question. Mr. Westinghouse agreed to employ him for two hours after school and all day on Saturdays, provided his grades did not suffer.

The pipe incident had sparked George's interest in steam power. He wanted to learn all he could about it. The Schenectady Free Library had a few books on the subject and he read every one. He also wrote letters to the companies manufacturing steam engines asking for technical pamphlets which they were glad to send.

The only engines in use were "reciprocating engines" like the one at G. Westinghouse & Co. These were large, clumsy machines in which steam was piped into a closed cylinder to move a heavy piston up and down. The steam entered and left the cylinder through a complicated valve arrange-

ment. The up-down movement was changed to circular
motion by means of a "piston rod" connecting the piston
to a long shaft. The shaft, by rotating, supplied power to
the machines through belts.

George saw immediately that reciprocating steam engines
were inefficient. Their bulk made them impractical for many
uses. The complicated connections needed to convert the
piston's up-down action into rotating motion wasted a good
deal of the power generated.

Why use a reciprocating engine to turn a shaft? he asked
himself. What if a different type of engine could be devised
that would convert steam power *directly* into rotary power?
It would be a giant step forward. No complicated mechanism
would be needed to translate the piston's up-down action
into circular motion, so there would be little waste of power.
And with fewer, less complicated parts, it would be cheaper
to build and less susceptible to mechanical breakdown.

Inspired by his vision, George was soon devoting all his
spare time to designing a rotary engine. In the months that
followed, he remained in a world of his own—a world
bounded by temperatures, steam pressures and control valves.
He always kept a pencil and paper handy and there was
scarcely a time when his parents would not find him hard
at work drawing imaginary engines of fantastic shapes and
complexity.

Before he finished a drawing, George usually crumpled
up the paper and threw it away, convinced he was not on
the right track. The problem was to find a substitute for
the straight action of the piston. If he did away with the
piston, how could he convert steam into mechanical power?
No matter how hard he tried, he could not come up with
a satisfactory substitute.

One blistering Sunday afternoon in June, 1860, George
set out to take a swim in the creek. It had rained heavily
the day before, and a large pool of water had collected on
high ground a hundred yards above the creek. The rain
water had found a passage to the lower level, and it was

trickling down along the rocks and rotted logs, gathering momentum until, at the juncture with the creek, it formed a tiny waterfall.

George studied this phenomenon as he started to take off his clothes. The trickling of the water into the creek reminded him of a waterfall he had once seen in a stream near Central Bridge at the site of a grain mill. The rapid current had been used to turn a huge paddle wheel which supplied power to the mill.

Suddenly an idea struck him. If water could turn a paddle wheel, why couldn't steam be used for the same purpose? Expanding steam had enormous power—power enough to drive a heavy piston in a cylinder back and forth. Indeed this was the principle of the reciprocating engine. There was no reason why it couldn't turn a paddle wheel instead. George paused with a shoe in his hand, transfixed by his vision. Why couldn't he devise a bladed wheel housed in a cylinder that would utilize the water wheel principle? By piping steam into the cylinder and directing it against the blades the wheel would spin. He could connect a round shaft to the center of the rotating wheel and the shaft would then turn with the wheel. For a moment he was stunned by the amazing simplicity of it. Why it was the very principle he had been searching for—an efficient, uncomplicated method of turning steam power into rotary mechanical power *directly*, without the wasteful intermediate step of converting the straight action of a piston into circular motion.

He spent the next months designing his rotary engine. He prepared drawings to scale, showing every detail of the mechanism. By late winter of 1861, the fourteen-year-old inventor was ready to begin construction of an experimental model. He asked his father for permission to return to the machine shop each evening after supper to work on his engine. Mr. Westinghouse, won over by his son's enthusiasm, consented. But George had barely gotten started when something happened that made him forget about the rotary engine for the time being.

On April 12, 1861, Southern forces attacked Union troops
at Fort Sumter, South Carolina, and fired shots whôse echoes
were to be heard for the next four years. Civil War had
broken out!

Like many Yankees from New England George Westinghouse, Sr., hated slavery. He was an ardent supporter of the
lanky, humble rail splitter from Illinois who had just taken
office as President. He had voted for Abraham Lincoln and
backed him in his declaration that the Union must be
preserved at all costs. However, with many other Northern-
ers he shared the illusion that the South would be defeated
in short order.

All the Westinghouse boys echoed their father's political
sentiments. But the most ardent patriot of all was young
George. He eagerly followed the newspaper accounts of the
fighting and dreamed adolescent dreams of performing heroic
deeds on imaginary battlefields.

One evening he came across a press story of a young
drummer boy from Philadelphia who had fallen while charg-
ing bravely into smoking Southern muskets. He read and
reread the account, and his eyes brimmed with tears. Finally
he tore the clipping out of the newspaper and put it in his
pocket.

The next day, during noon recess at school, he showed
the article to Thomas Hill, a classmate. Like George, young
Hill had overly romantic notions about war and fancied
himself in uniform sharing the glories of battle. By the end
of the afternoon the two youths had agreed on a daring
scheme.

The next morning, just before dawn, George slipped out
of bed, emptied his bank of ten dollars he had saved out
of his wages, and climbed down the trellis leading from his
room. He padded silently across the lawn and raced down
the darkened street. The sun was just climbing over a dark
pink horizon when he met Tom Hill at the corner of Union
and State streets.

"Do you have your train fare?" Tom asked.

"Yes, ten dollars," George replied, breathless from his exertions.

Hill's face fell. "Will we have enough? I have only five."

George nodded. "Of course. All we need do is to pay our way to New York City. Then we'll be in the Army and have no need to spend our own money."

The boys started walking down the street toward the railroad station. Tom Hill stopped.

"What's the matter now?" George demanded.

"What will we tell the Army when we are asked our ages?" Tom said in a hoarse, anxious whisper.

"Why, we'll say we're eighteen, of course," George told him impatiently. "We're both tall. I'm almost six feet and you—well you're tall enough to be a man."

As they approached the station, Tom's uncertainty increased. He wondered if they were acting too hastily, but George continued to reassure him. At the terminal they did not go near the ticket office but loitered in the freight area where they were certain they would not be spotted.

"The important thing is not to buy the tickets at the station, but to wait until we're on the train and buy them from the trainmaster," George explained. "That way no one will know we plan to leave."

The long wait made them hungry. Tom opened a tin of biscuits he had filched from his mother's pantry the night before and they ate in silence.

At eight-thirty they heard the rumble of the train in the distance. It crawled into the station and came to a slow, uneven stop. The conspirators looked about cautiously, then scrambled aboard the last coach. It was empty except for three or four dozing passengers. They took a seat up front. After fifteen minutes of anxious waiting, they heard the trainmaster's signal for the train to leave. They held their breath.

"George! Tom Hill!"

The voice was familiar. George got a sinking feeling in the pit of his stomach.

"I think you'd better come home with me!" George
Westinghouse, Sr., strode up the aisle of the coach and
crooked a finger at the two runaways. Without a word they
got up, followed him sheepishly off the train and walked
silently from the station.

At home, Mr. Westinghouse sat George in a chair and
said quietly, "War is a terrible thing, and I hope this one
does not go on much longer. If it does, and you are old
enough to know what you are doing, I will give you my
permission. But not until then. Do you understand?"

George nodded respectfully.

"Very well," his father said glancing at his pocket watch.
"It's time for you to get ready for school."

At the door, George paused. "Father?"

"Yes."

"How did you know Tom Hill and I ran away?"

The father pursed his lips to keep from grinning. "The
stationmaster saw you when you boarded the train and sent
for me," he explained. "Now we'll say nothing more about
what happened this morning. Is that understood?"

"Yes, sir," George said.

Mr. Westinghouse was as good as his word. He never men-
tioned the incident again.

During the next two years the rotary engine was almost
forgotten as George followed the bloody fighting with youthful intensity. In 1862 his older brother Albert joined the
New York Volunteer Cavalry and was commissioned a lieutenant. Then John joined the Navy.

By September, 1863, George could no longer be held back,
and though he was only seventeen years old his father reluctantly gave him permission to enlist.

3

Man on a Train

GEORGE PACKED A BAG HURRIEDLY AND TOOK A TRAIN TO NEW
York City. The next morning he was sworn into the United
States Army as a private. Given a choice he selected the
cavalry, just as Albert had.

Almost at once he began to have second thoughts about
the wisdom of choosing that branch of the service. He had
imagined Army life would be an adventurous lark and was
disappointed to learn it consisted largely of drilling under
a broiling sun and crawling in the mud on back-breaking
training exercises. The food was beans and hardtack soaked
in frying-pan grease to make them edible.

He also discovered to his dismay that a cavalryman had
the added responsibility of caring for his horse—even before
he could eat or rest himself. Frequently it meant foraging
for grass or fodder until long after dark and returning to the
campfire half-starved only to find that most of the company
rations had been eaten.

When the initial training period was over, George's company was sent to the rolling hills of northern Virginia on
picket duty. It was a quiet area. Skirmishes with the enemy
were few and far between. The opportunity for glory was
almost nonexistent. The company's main task was to guard
against spies and the possibility that occasional Rebel raid-

ing parties might try to pierce the Union lines. After two months George was bored and homesick.

But in December the unit received a pleasant surprise. All the men were to be furloughed for the Christmas holidays! George wrote his parents the good news. He was delighted to learn that his brothers John and Albert were to receive holiday leaves, too. It was agreed that Mr. and Mrs. Westinghouse were to come down from Schenectady and all were to meet in New York City for a family reunion.

George took a train from Washington and was met in New York by his grinning brothers and his parents. Mr. Westinghouse pumped his hand. His mother hugged him and wept.

They took a horse carriage to the home of one of Mrs. Westinghouse's aunts for dinner. She lived in a fine house on the outskirts of the city. When they arrived, Albert, who had given the aunt's house as the place where he could be reached in an emergency, found a message waiting for him. His leave had been canceled! He was to report at once to military headquarters in City Hall Park and be prepared to depart with his unit.

Solemnly Albert kissed his mother, shook hands with his father and brothers and climbed back into the carriage. As the horse clattered down the road, he leaned out and waved a final good-by.

Albert's leaving dampened the spirit of the reunion. Nevertheless the rest of the family talked far into the night. In an attempt to lighten the evening, George and John tried to regale their parents with amusing anecdotes about army life.

George told them about the night he had been on guard duty and had heard a sudden rustling of bushes behind him. In a quaking voice he had ordered the intruder to halt, only to receive a loud whinny in reply. "It was the captain's horse!" he explained with a laugh. Then John told about a young seaman who'd been told to drill a group of naval recruits on board ship. The sailor had forgotten the order for reverse march and had almost marched his men over the side!

Although Mr. and Mrs. Westinghouse made a gallant effort to laugh with their sons at these humorous experiences it was clear that in spirit they were with Albert who was undoubtedly on his way to battle.

Early in 1864 President Lincoln turned over to a little known general named Ulysses S. Grant command of the Union forces. Grant immediately launched a campaign to cut the Confederacy in two. At last it was beginning to look as if the war would be won in the foreseeable future, but George's unit remained on picket duty in the quiet hills of northern Virginia.

In April he arrived at an important decision: he would apply for a transfer to the Navy! The commanding officer of his cavalry unit listened thoughtfully to his plea and agreed to give him a pass to Washington to submit the necessary applications.

Naval headquarters was a beehive of activity and seeming confusion.

"Why do you want to be transferred?" he was asked.

"Because I have had training as a mechanic," he explained candidly. "I feel I could serve my country better by drawing on that experience."

He described the work he had done in his father's shop and answered questions put to him by a young naval engineer assigned to test his knowledge of mechanics.

"It seems you have acquired a good deal of information and experience, Westinghouse," the officer said briskly. "Particularly about steam engines. Very well, I think the Navy can use you."

A week later George's transfer came through. He was assigned as a third assistant engineer aboard the *Muscoota*, a steam-powered gunboat on blockade duty with the Potomac Flotilla.

The moment he set foot in the engine room below decks,

he felt at home. To be near machinery once again lifted his spirits and seemed to cancel out the memory of the boring months he had spent as a cavalry soldier. He set right to work to learn all he could about marine engineering. Actually the *Muscoota*'s engine was not too different in principle from the steam engines used on land to power machinery. Soon he knew more about the ship's mechanical operation than any of his crewmates.

During the quiet hours off duty, George's active mind turned once again to his long-delayed project to construct a rotary engine. It was more than two years since he had completed the plans, but he still believed in his idea. He asked permission of the chief engineer to use the ship's lathe and tools during his free time. The officer, who had taken a liking to George, gave his approval.

While most of his shipmates spent their off-duty time gambling or relating exaggerated stories about their shore-leave adventures, George was busy machining the parts for his small experimental engine. One day the ship's carpenter —a burly man of fifty named Hanson—asked him what he was working on. George showed him the plans for the rotary engine and explained its functioning.

Hanson, a fine workman with superbly skilled hands, was impressed. "I see the advantage of such an engine," he declared scratching his chin thoughtfully. "But will it work?"

"I think so," George replied as he carefully filed the tiny blades for the rotating wheel. "We'll know for sure when I test it."

"How will you test it?"

George paused. He hadn't as yet given serious thought to the problem of testing the mechanism, but Hanson had raised an important point. It was one thing for the engine to rotate, another for it to generate enough power to be of practical use. So he admitted sheepishly, "Frankly, Mr. Hanson, I've completely overlooked the matter."

"Wait a minute, lad, and perhaps I can be of help," Hanson replied. He left the shop and went to his cabin. A few minutes later he was back carrying a three-foot-long wooden model of a sloop-of-war which he showed to George with pride.

"Made it myself. It's scaled perfectly—down to the inch. Took me over two months. I have three or four others in my cabin."

George admired the little ship. It was a beautiful piece of work, so perfectly made that even the rudder moved when the tiny wheel on the bridge was turned.

"How would you like to test your engine on this vessel?" Hanson said. "We can convert it into a sidewheeler and give your design a real test."

George was delighted and agreed readily to the generous proposal. When he completed the rotary model, he showed Hanson how it should be installed in the ship. The skilled carpenter did the job in two days. He left a small opening near the stern so fuel could be fed into the tiny furnace to heat up the boiler.

The next time the *Muscoota* docked in Washington for stores and the crew was given leave, George and the carpenter brought the model on shore. They found a small protected inlet at the edge of the Potomac. George tied a ball of string to the stern, fired up the tiny boiler and set the vessel in the water. In less than a minute the tiny paddle wheel began to turn. It turned slowly at first, then faster until it churned water. The small vessel began to move. George played out the string excitedly.

"Look at her speed, Mr. Hanson!" he shouted. "Why she's moving so fast I can't let out line fast enough."

"Aye, George. Your engine is a success."

Hanson wore a big grin. Then he warned, "Look out! She's beginning to ship water."

George had set the rudder so the vessel would traverse a large circle. Now, because of her speed and the weight of the paddle wheel and engine, she was listing badly to starboard. Water was streaming into the hold. Suddenly the engine sputtered and died.

"The water must have put out the fire," George muttered.

They hauled in the little ship and emptied her. However, moisture remained in the fire box, and they could not get the fire started again. So they headed back for the *Muscoota*.

"Well, there are some parts to be improved, but at least the engine works," George declared happily as they walked along.

"What will you do with the contraption?" Hanson wanted to know.

"I don't know yet," the young man mused. "Apply for a patent after the war is over, I suppose. My father has a number of patents for improvements he's made on threshers and other farm equipment. I'll ask him to help me prepare the documents."

"Well, good luck to you, lad," the amicable carpenter replied. "Now, how about a mug of ale to celebrate?"

Shortly afterward, George was transferred to the *Stars and Stripes,* another steam vessel in the Potomac Flotilla. He was sorry to leave the *Muscoota,* for he liked Hanson. As a parting gift, the carpenter presented him with the model sloop-of-war.

"Take good care of it," Hanson said. "It's a token of esteem from an old sailor who is convinced you'll go far."

Early in 1865 George received a tragic letter from his mother, informing him that Albert had been killed while leading a charge against the Confederates in Louisiana. She wrote: "We did not know when your brother was recalled to duty during our reunion in New York City that we would never see him again. Albert died a hero. That knowledge will not bring him back, my son, but perhaps it will give us strength in the trying days ahead."

That night George sobbed into his pillow, not really caring whether his shipmates heard him or not.

On April 9, 1865, in the court house at Appomattox, Virginia, General Robert E. Lee presented his sword in surrender to General Ulysses Grant. Seventeen days later, Con-

federate General Johnston followed Lee's lead and surren-
dered to the Union forces. The war was over.

George accepted the victory solemnly, waiting to be discharged from the Navy. The news of Albert's death had
created a great guilt in him. For while Albert had fought
and died on the bloody battlefields of Louisiana, he, George
—the most vociferous patriot of all—had spent the last two
years safe from enemy bullets.

It had not been a matter of personal choice of course.
Moreover, the Potomac Flotilla, by participating in the successful blockading of Southern ports, had played its own
important part in the defeat of the Confederacy. Yet George
could not help wondering why it was Albert rather than
he who had been fated to die. At nineteen, he was concerned for the first time with the enigma of death.

For this reason George Westinghouse was not in a happy
frame of mind as he traveled up the Hudson by train on the
sun-drenched afternoon of June 15, 1865. He had just been
discharged from the Navy and was going home. It should
have been a time of rejoicing, but instead he felt moody,
pensive. The encounter that morning with the old man
who had lost a son at Nashville had not helped. Indeed it
had served to reinforce the depression that had taken hold
of him in recent months.

George listened to the determined chug-chugging of the
locomotive up ahead and wondered if they would arrive on
schedule. Usually the train was several hours late. He glanced
out of the window and saw that the sun was beginning to lie
low in the west. In another hour or so it would be dark.

He was starting to feel sleepy now, so he stretched out his
long legs as best he could and closed his eyes. Just as he was
about to doze off, there was a sharp grinding noise followed
by a sickening jolt that hurled him out of his seat.

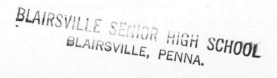

4

The Inventor

GEORGE FOUND HIMSELF SPRAWLED IN THE MIDDLE OF THE aisle. He was shaken but unhurt, as were the other passengers. Outside there was shouting and excitement. George got to his feet and lifted one of the grimy windows. "What happened?" he called out to a grease-stained brakeman who was hurrying along carrying a heavy crowbar.

"Derailed car up front!" the brakeman shouted. "Nothing to worry about, sir."

"Nothing to worry about, indeed!" an elderly lady across the aisle grumbled. "Why, we all could have been killed."

A middle-aged man agreed vigorously. "You're absolutely right, madam! These trains are a disgrace. We'll probably be here all night."

George hurried to the end of the coach, opened the door and jumped down from the car platform. The brakeman's report was accurate. The tender just behind the locomotive had jumped the track.

He stood by and watched as the train's crew, under the trainmaster's supervision, put huge crowbars under the wheels of the tender and struggled to inch it back toward the track. It was slow, backbreaking work. Finally George asked if he could help.

"That you can," a sweating brakeman groaned, as he strained at the end of one of the heavy iron bars. "You're a big fellow and you look like you've plenty of muscle. Just

44

take hold of this crowbar and tug when I do. Aye, that's a good lad."

For the next two hours George helped the train crew edge the heavy tender closer to the track. It was a hot night and they had to stop frequently to catch their breath. By the time the car was in position for the final hoist onto the track, he was close to exhaustion and his clothes were wringing wet.

"All right, men," the trainmaster shouted. "This final lift will be the hardest. Rest up a bit first."

George and the brakeman laid down the crowbar and mopped their faces. "Are trains derailed often?" he asked.

"More often than you'd think," replied the railroad worker. "See that rail there? That's the culprit. She must have loosened." He pointed to a section of track just behind the locomotive where two men with sledge hammers were pounding heavy spikes into the wooden ties.

George nodded. Even to his inexperienced eye it was clear that one of the rails had become loose and separated from the rest of the track.

"But the locomotive is ahead of the tender," George said in a puzzled tone. "Why didn't it jump the track, too?"

"Because the engine is heavier," the brakeman explained patiently. "Sometimes, though, a heavy car'll do the same, if she's going too fast."

George rubbed his chin thoughtfully. If derailings were indeed a common occurrence, he wondered why no one had devised a more efficient way to replace derailed cars. His musings were interrupted by the trainmaster's hoarse voice. "All right. The loose rail is repaired. Let's get this car back on the track!"

The men placed the long iron bars under the wheels of the tender again and heaved in unison. The car moved almost imperceptibly. The trainmaster continued to shout words of encouragement. "Good work, men! The next try will do it."

They heaved again. The derailed car rose, hovered in the air and slid onto the track. The sweating workers cheered.

While the train crew recoupled the tender to the rest of

the train, George's brain was working at a furious pace. Why couldn't mechanical power be used to replace derailed cars? he asked himself.

His memory traveled back to that summer afternoon in his father's shop seven years ago when he had devised a method of utilizing steam power to cut the iron pipes for the new threshing machines. It occurred to him that this problem was not unlike the earlier one. He stared at the huge locomotive. In the moonlight it looked like a ghostly gray dragon as its giant stack belched forth great puff clouds of black smoke.

Steam power! Why the power was right there—in the locomotive itself. George felt a sense of exultation. Now if only it could be harnessed to *pull* a derailed car back on the track!

His mind was running on at a furious excited pace, but as his thoughts progressed they followed a precise and logical pattern. Suppose a pair of mobile rails were placed in front of the wheels of a derailed car, he pondered. Suppose too, that the other ends of these rails were connected to permanent track. Why couldn't the engine then be hitched up to the derailed car and used to pull it back to the track? It would be like switching a train from one track to another.

Yes, such a plan might just work. He described it to the brakeman. "Why, it would cut down the time of replacing a car from two hours to about fifteen minutes," he predicted.

The railroad worker looked dubious and scratched his stubbled chin. "I wouldn't know about machines and such. I'm just a brakeman. The idea seems simple enough, but you're mighty young—no disrespect meant to the uniform you wear, lad—to be knowing more about railroading than the bewhiskered gentlemen who operate this line."

Refusing to be discouraged, George spent the rest of the trip drawing diagrams of oddly shaped railroad tracks. Since he had no paper, he used the back of his Navy orders for his sketches.

Mr. and Mrs. Westinghouse and his brothers and sisters

greeted him joyfully. For the next week he did little but sleep and enjoy his mother's expert cooking, for she'd made up her mind that the Navy had starved him and she was determined "to put the meat back on his bones."

George returned to work at G. Westinghouse & Co. at the end of July, his brain buzzing with plans for the car replacer. When the regular working day was over, he hurried home for dinner, then went back to the shop at night to work on the scale model of the new device. In addition, and with his father's help, he completed the documents needed to apply for a patent for his rotary engine.

One Sunday afternoon toward the end of August, Mr. Westinghouse asked George to join him for a walk. "Well, son, now that you're home safe and have had a chance to see what civil life is like, what are your plans?" he asked matter-of-factly.

George thought for a moment. "I want to be an inventor, Father."

"A what?"

"An inventor. I want to invent things. I think I have a knack for it, but more important, it's what I want to do most in the world. The car replacer I've told you about, for instance—I think I could sell it to the railroads."

Mr. Westinghouse paused, turned to his son and stared at him for a long moment. "George, I'm going to be perfectly frank. You've always had pretty much your own way. You're a man now and you've just been through a war so I don't presume to tell you now how to live your life. But I do think you're not looking at things realistically. If you like inventing, well and good. I have a few patents myself, as you know. However, you can't support yourself as an inventor because it's a risky business at best. An invention may succeed, but it's more likely that it will fail. If it's gambling you like, why you stand as good a chance of winning in a gaming hall. Take this replacer device, or whatever you call it. What do you know of railroading? Nothing. There are men who have spent their lives at it, yet you would presume to say that

you have succeeded where they have failed? It's—well, it's
downright pigheadedness, that's what it is!"

George kicked a pebble with the toe of his shoe and stared
down at the glassy waters of the Erie Canal. A light mist
hovered over the city and off in the distance a canal boat blew
a long sad note on her horn. He thought about what his
father had just said, particularly about the car replacer. It
was curious how much Mr. Westinghouse's words sounded
like those of the brakeman. In effect, both had said the same
thing—that he was young and knew nothing about railroading and should leave such matters to the elderly gentlemen
who ran the railroads.

It occurred to George that they were both about the same
age, his father and the railroad worker, men in their fifties,
and that what they had said about the car replacer represented
their over-all philosophy toward life. It was the cautious outlook of age, the conservatism of men who had lived and
witnessed failure and disappointment, both in their own
lives and in the lives of others.

But he, George Westinghouse, Jr., was only nineteen—
not fifty! How could he explain to men of an older genera-
tion that the world had changed since their youth? He had
just been through the Civil War, and he had seen the great
changes wrought by the war and sensed the restless spirit of
progress that had risen out of the immense tragedy to kindle
the hearts and minds of the nation's youth.

In all the fields of human endeavor men were forging
ahead. In medicine, through the discovery of anesthesia,
doctors had found a way to deaden pain before surgery and
thus extend the boundaries of human life. Across the land
other pioneers had stretched a singing wire over which telegraph messages could be sent from coast to coast. Now there
was talk of a continuous railroad line that would span the
continent and hasten the conquest of the western frontier.
And at that moment, too, a great vessel was plowing the
surging waters of the North Atlantic in an effort to lay an

undersea cable from North America to Europe that would bring all the civilized peoples of the world closer together.

How could he explain to his father that he wanted to be part of that new world—to serve in the ranks of those dedicated to making the visions of a better life for all humanity come true? In truth he knew it could not be done. For they were of different generations, he and his father, separated by a gulf in age and outlook that could never be bridged.

George said, "I appreciate what you're trying to tell me, Father. Perhaps you're right. But I must try things my own way first. If I fail—well, at least I'll have tried. The failure will be my own."

"You've always been a willful lad," Mr. Westinghouse said. "I suppose you inherited it from me. I can't force you to change your mind, but I do want you to listen to a proposal. I am willing to pay your way through Union College here in Schenectady if you will agree to enroll. They have a fine mechanical course, and there is still time to be accepted for the fall semester."

George was quite unprepared for such an offer. He thought hard for a moment. "But I'm nineteen," he said finally. "The other students will be two or three years younger. At my age I must begin to stand on my own two feet. It's a question of self-respect. No, Father, I appreciate your kindness, but I can't accept."

They walked along in silence. Then Mr. Westinghouse, his eyes misty, quietly said, "There's one more thing I want to add, George. All these years our greatest ambition—your mother's and mine—has been to see our sons get a college education. The war just about dashed our hopes. Jay and John are too old now, and Albert—well, poor Albert is dead, though he was the one who was most truly desirous of going to college. Herman is still too young for college, but every day he shows promise of being more and more like you."

George knew what his father was trying to say. He was asking *him* to take Albert's place. The mental image of Albert buried under a white cross in a Louisiana clay field moved him deeply, and the guilt which had plagued him since the news of Albert's death resurged stronger than ever.

"I—I'd like to think about your offer, Father," he said hesitantly, his resolve shaken by Mr. Westinghouse's words.

That night at dinner he announced his decision to enroll in college for the fall semester.

Union was a small institution with one hundred and ninety students, all men. It was located in the heart of Schenectady where a Gothic-spired library building sat like a jeweled crown in the middle of the campus. George was admitted to the college on September 15, 1865, as a student in the scientific department. Because of his age and the mechanical knowledge he had gleaned through extensive reading and his naval experience, the dean put him in the sophomore class. Even as a second year student he was way ahead of the others. The classes in engineering were so elementary that he felt he could put the time to better use by working on his car replacer. So he began to cut classes regularly. In a few weeks he succeeded in compiling a notorious attendance record. It came to the attention of the head of the scientific department, and George was summoned to his office and warned. He promised not to miss classes again even though it meant putting aside the car replacer for the time being.

In addition to the courses in mechanics he was required to take French, German, mathematics and English. He got good grades in mathematics and English, but when it came to foreign languages, he was lost. Nevertheless for a time he made a sincere effort to apply himself to his studies.

In November, however, he received exciting news. A patent had been granted on his rotary steam engine! This initial success as an inventor put an end to his good intentions. The temptation to resume work on the car replacer proved too strong, and he slipped back into his old habit of cutting classes.

Shortly before the Christmas holidays he was called in by the acting president of the college, Dr. Hickok. The educator, a tall, spare man, cleared his throat and shuffled through some papers on his desk. Then he stared at George through gold-rimmed spectacles. "Westinghouse, do you like our college?" he asked calmly.

"Yes, sir. I think Union is a fine school," George replied.

"Then why do you miss out on the educational opportunities we have to offer? Your attendance record is the worst I've ever seen."

George hesitated for a moment. "May I speak frankly, sir?"

"Please do," Dr. Hickok told him.

"Union is an excellent institution, but I don't think it is for me. I'm bored here."

Dr. Hickok raised his eyebrows. "Go on, Westinghouse," he said. "I'm interested, particularly since I'm told that you have a fine mind for science and mechanics."

For the next half hour George spoke candidly about his hopes and dreams for the future. He told about his rotary engine and his plan for a car replacer and how he had always found it difficult to adjust to the discipline of classroom studies.

Dr. Hickok listened intently. When George had finished, the college president stared up at the ceiling thoughtfully. Then he spoke in slow, measured tones. "Westinghouse, I am glad you've talked as you did, for I know a good deal more about you now than when you walked in here a short time ago. I intend to speak just as frankly. I think you are right in stating that Union College is not for you. Every so often we educators run across a student who finds the classroom atmosphere stultifying. That is not to say that such young men are mentally incapable of doing college work. On the contrary, often they are brilliant, and it is their very brilliance that causes them to stifle in the necessarily rigid discipline of the lecture hall. They are—well, we think of them as square pegs in round academic holes. I honestly think you are one of those 'square pegs,' Westinghouse. It is nothing to be ashamed of, and indeed, I have no fears for your future. You have only my best wishes for your success."

"Thank you, Dr. Hickok," George said quietly.

That evening he told his parents about his interview with the president. The next day Mr. Westinghouse paid a visit to the school and was closeted with Dr. Hickok for over an hour.

At the end of the Christmas holidays George did not return to Union College.

But his escape from the confining influence of higher education was not without its cost. George was aware that in winning his point he had thwarted his father's ambitions for him. Still overcome by grief at the death of Albert, George, Sr. said nothing, but his son sensed his hurt. Albert would never have gone contrary to his father's wishes—George knew that for a certainty. Now, instead of easing his parents' burden he had added to their mental anguish, as he had done all his life. It was not a pleasant thought to live with.

Sometimes at night he would dream that Albert was still alive and would wake up in a cold sweat in the darkness of his room. It was almost as if his dead brother were returning to reproach him for making their father unhappy. It was not easy to compete with the dead, and soon he was caught up in the ridiculous game of comparing himself to his brother and trying to convince himself that in his own way he was just as good a son as Albert had been. Consciously he knew it was a silly, childish thing to do, and yet the need was there to rid himself of the sense of guilt that hung over him like a specter.

It was this very feeling of inadequacy that soon led to a burning desire within to make a success of himself. All his life he had failed, he told himself—as a student, as a son, even in his military career—and now he decided that he would have to succeed at something, and for the moment it didn't matter too much at what. So in desperation he grasped at the nearest goal at hand: building his car replacer.

What had been an interesting project before, now became an obsession. He began to work at his invention with a

furious sense of determination. Freed from the rigid schedule of college classes and study assignments, he began to
devote all his evenings to completing a working model. Days,
he worked at his old job at G. Westinghouse & Co. as a
salaried mechanic.

The final design for the device was so devastatingly simple
that George wondered why no one had thought of it before.
It consisted simply of a pair of rails with clamps at the ends
so they could be run off from the track at an angle. In this
respect it was like a "frog"—a section of railway track where
one rail diverges from another so trains can be switched. By
bringing the rails of the replacer up even against the wheels
of the nearest derailed car, an engine could be hitched to
the car to pull it back onto the track.

Even Mr. Westinghouse, who had a keen mechanical mind,
was impressed with the finished model. "I must confess it
looks as if it can do the job," he told his son, fingering the
tiny cars George had placed on the tracks to demonstrate
how the replacer was to be used. "What will the device be
made of—cast iron?"

"No, Father," the youth replied. "Something more durable.
Steel. Cast steel."

Mr. Westinghouse was astonished. "I'm not a railroad
man, George, but I do know that frogs and equipment of
that kind are always made of cast iron."

"That's true," George admitted. "But I've been down to
the railroad yards talking to the workmen, and one of the
things I've found is that cast iron does not stand up under
severe use. As a result equipment has to be replaced often.
Now there's a company—the Bessemer Steel Works in Troy
—that has developed a method of making steel castings which
will outlast iron many times."

Warming up to his subject he explained he had also gotten the idea of making railroad frogs out of cast steel. "What's
more, Father, I can make a frog that's reversible, so when
one side is worn out it can be turned over! It will reduce
the railroad's cost considerably."

Mr. Westinghouse said wryly, "And how do you intend to finance these elaborate projects, George?"

The youth hesitated. "Well, I'd thought that you—"

George, Sr., shook his head vigorously. "My ready funds are tied up in the company. Besides, I know nothing about railroading, and I've always held that a man's a fool to invest in a business he knows nothing about. . . ."

George's face fell.

". . . But I'll *lend* you a little money to cover the patent costs and incidental expenses," Mr. Westinghouse added with a smile. "After all, I do owe it to my son to show that I still have faith in him."

George spent the next month trying to secure financial backing. He visited the offices of prominent Schenectady businessmen with the replacer model. Most of them knew his father and received him cordially, but like Mr. Westinghouse they knew nothing about railroading and had no desire to sink money into a project they did not understand.

At last he was referred to a real estate investor named Rawls. A small gray-haired man with shrewd, penetrating eyes, Rawls toyed with the replacer model but said nothing for a full five minutes.

Suddenly he slammed his fist against the top of his desk and announced dramatically, "All right, Westinghouse, you've sold me on your idea. I'll put five thousand dollars of my own into the venture, and I'll get a friend, Hubert Wall, to put in another five thousand. We'll form a company with a three-way partnership."

George was delighted and began to thank the real estate man, but Rawls held up his hand. "Not so fast, young man. In return we'll expect you to assign the royalties from your replacer and frog to our company. You will also have to serve as our salesman."

The youthful inventor agreed eagerly to these terms.

In four months the firm of Rawls, Wall and Westinghouse was a going concern. George made a trip to Troy with his blueprints and worked out an agreement to have the castings

of the replacer and reversible frogs made at the Bessemer
Steel Works. By early fall he was on the road carrying
models of the equipment and freshly printed business cards
identifying himself as "George Westinghouse, Chief Salesman."

His first stop was at the Chicago offices of the Chicago,
Burlington and Quincy Railroad. A local banker in Schenectady had suggested that he write to the superintendent of
the road, a man named Towne, to ask for an appointment.
George had done so and enclosed diagrams of his inventions.
In return he had received a cordial note from Superintendent Towne inviting him to call at his office.

The railroad official was a tall, lanky man of about fifty
with alert gray eyes and a friendly smile. He studied the
models thoughtfully and said, "Mr. Westinghouse, there's
no need to waste time. I've examined the diagrams you sent
and I'm impressed with the equipment. In fact, I'm prepared
to sign a contract for two replacers and two frogs. If they
work well there'll be an order for more."

George was flabbergasted. The entire transaction had
taken no more than ten minutes!

He left Superintendent Towne's office walking on air. His
first prospect—his first sale! By the time he reached the street
he was fully convinced that it was no trick at all to achieve
success in business.

5

Marguerite

GEORGE WAS ON THE ROAD CONTINUALLY IN THE NEXT FEW months. Having made the sale to the Chicago, Burlington and Quincy he had no trouble getting appointments with officials of the other roads. Superintendent Towne was respected by his colleagues, and mention of the fact that he had purchased Rawls, Wall and Westinghouse equipment whetted their interest.

Soon orders were coming in so fast that the Bessemer Steel Works could not keep up with them. George contracted with a second steel company in Pompton, New Jersey, to do the casting for some of the replacers and frogs.

Returning from a visit to the New Jersey plant one day he boarded a Hudson River Railroad train in New York City. It was crowded with passengers, but he finally located a vacant seat in the last car, next to an uncommonly pretty girl.

She was about nineteen, with dark hair, a creamy complexion, and lovely blue eyes that reminded George of a cloudless autumn sky. He wanted to strike up a conversation immediately but fearing she would think him too forward, pretended to bury himself in a book on steam engineering.

However, as the train left the yard it rounded a sharp bend with a lurch. The girl was thrown against him. She apologized blushingly.

56

"That's quite all right," he said with a smile. "That curve is a bad one. Someday they'll retrack it."

"You seem to know this line well," she said. "Do you travel it often?"

"Quite a bit," he replied in a blasé manner. "You see, I'm connected with railroading."

"Oh, that sounds exciting."

Soon they were chatting amiably. George found himself telling her about his inventions and how he expected every railroad to be equipped with his car replacers in the near future. The girl listened attentively and asked him a great many questions about his work. He told her he hoped someday to be a full-time inventor.

"Then you don't intend to remain a salesman?" she asked.

"Definitely not," he declared. "My main interest is inventing things, not selling them."

She said, "I've never met an inventor before. Why does a person become one?"

He thought for a moment. "For the same reason, I suppose, that someone becomes an artist or a scientist or a musician. It's not primarily to make money. Inventing is something I *have* to do in spite of myself. . . ." He halted in embarrassment.

"No, go on," she urged gently. "I'm really fascinated."

"Well," he continued, "the need to invent is something you're born with, I guess. Most people, when they look at, say, a team of horses pulling a plow, are content to accept the situation as it is. That's the way it's done and that's the way it always will be done, they think. But an inventor—well, he looks at things differently. He's never content with things as they are. He'll see the horses pulling the plow and he'll ask himself: Isn't there an easier way, a more efficient way of doing it? And almost at once he tries to figure out a better way. Do you understand? Being an inventor is a state of mind —a way of looking at things."

"That's a wonderful explanation." Then she added with

a throaty laugh, "You make it sound as if inventors are essentially lazy people."

"In a way I suppose they are," he grinned. "They can't stand waste—whether it's time or energy. I would be willing to wager that every invention since the beginning of time was conceived by a lazy man."

"But aren't inventors interested in helping people, too?" she asked more seriously. "I imagine it's a great thrill to know you're making life easier for everyone."

He replied, "That's part of the satisfaction, all right. Up to now, of course, I haven't done anything really important, but it's every inventor's dream to create something that will revolutionize the lives of all people."

There was a brief lull in the conversation, and George realized with a start that while he had told the young lady all about his inventions, he knew very little about her. In fact they did not even know each other's names. So he introduced himself formally. She told him her name was Marguerite Erskine Walker, that she lived in Roxbury, New York, and she was on her way to Kingston to visit relatives.

She took out a lunch basket and shared sandwiches, fruit and a homemade cake with him. He told her the food was delicious, even though he had eaten a heavy meal in New York before boarding the train.

Just before they pulled into Rhinebeck where she was to change for the Kingston Ferry, George asked if he could see her again. She reddened but nodded a quick yes and gave him her address. He wrote it down in his pocket notebook.

When he arrived home in Schenectady that evening his mother asked him why he was in such high spirits. He replied simply, "Because I've met the girl I'm going to marry."

In the next few weeks George visited Marguerite several times in Kingston. Before they met he had not liked traveling about because it took him away from the shop, but now he saw that it had its advantages, too. Traveling gave him an opportunity to see the girl whereas it would have been almost impossible if his work had confined him to Schenectady.

When Marguerite returned to Roxbury, George called at her home to meet her parents. On his third visit he carried a modest little ring.

That evening they sat on the porch although there was a crispness in the air. The night was clear, and high above the moon and the stars shone down benevolently.

"Marguerite," George said, swallowing hard, "I want you to have something." He fumbled clumsily in his pockets and took out the ring. His heart was thumping so loudly he hoped she couldn't hear it. "It's an engagement ring," he said. "Will you wear it?"

Her eyes shone. "Yes," she said, and slipped the ring on her finger.

"I haven't much to offer right now," he said half apologetically. "It will be some time before the company shows a real profit, so I can't promise you a house or nice furniture for the present. But I do have high hopes for the future, and if you are willing to share it with me as my wife I'll be proud and happy."

"Yes, oh yes, George," the girl murmured, "I do want to marry you."

On August 8, 1867, George Westinghouse, Jr., and Miss Marguerite Erskine Walker were married at the home of the bride's parents in Roxbury, New York. There was no time for an extended honeymoon because the groom had to be in Chicago on business. And since they could not afford a home of their own, Mr. and Mrs. Westinghouse insisted that the young couple stay with them for the time being, an offer which they accepted gratefully.

When George boarded the train for Chicago, Marguerite remained behind in Schenectady. His appointment was with officials of two of the smaller railroad lines, and he had no trouble convincing them to sign contracts for car replacers. Afterward, though he was eager to rush back to Schenectady, he found that the next train east did not leave for three hours. So he decided to drop in on Superintendent Towne in the Chicago, Burlington and Quincy yards to find out how the new equipment was working out.

The railroad executive was cordial, yet George couldn't help sensing that he was worried about something.

"Is anything wrong, Mr. Towne?" he inquired. "Wasn't the last shipment of equipment satisfactory?"

"No, no, Westinghouse, the replacers and frogs are splendid," the superintendent assured him. "It's not that at all. In fact I wish our other problems could be solved so easily."

"Problems, sir?"

"Braking," Towne told him. "The problem of how to stop our trains."

"I don't quite understand," George said.

The superintendent held up a sheaf of papers. "These are reports of accidents on the Chicago, Burlington and Quincy. Five—all in the space of one month. Fortunately no one was killed and only three persons were injured, but mark my words, one day there will be a serious accident and then there'll be the devil to pay."

George listened eagerly. "What sort of accidents were they, Mr. Towne?" he asked.

"Various kinds. Two derailments, two minor collisions and one mishap where the engineer couldn't slow down while rounding a curve so a passenger was thrown off a seat. None of these would have happened if we had an efficient braking system for our trains."

"Do other railroads face the same problem?" George inquired, his interest aroused.

"All of them. There isn't a railroad man in this country who wouldn't give his right arm for a reliable method of stopping and slowing down trains. It's what we've been dreaming about for years. Come here, let me show you something."

George followed Towne to his desk and watched as the

older man spread out a huge map of the United States, veined with black lines.

"This map shows all the railroads in this country," the superintendent explained. "Only two years ago—at the end of the war—there were something like thirty-five thousand miles of operating track on all the roads. Today there are nearly fifty thousand. And you know of course that the Union Pacific is building a road that will span the continent, coast to coast. Why at this rate we'll have more than a hundred and fifty thousand miles of track in less than twenty years."

George nodded silently.

The railroad official was speaking with intensity now and the words poured out in a torrent. "The railroads are the rivers of steel that can turn this country of ours into a land of milk and honey. They can extend the frontier and bring an army of settlers to the West. They can encourage industry and expand commerce. Why, the railroads can make us the greatest nation on the face of the earth!"

George was hypnotized by the word picture Superintendent Towne was painting. He envisioned great cities dotting the countryside. He saw vast quantities of manufactured goods and raw materials piled high on railroad cars speeding along gleaming rails that ribboned the land in all directions. He visualized trains crowded with men and women and children crossing the arid prairies in a matter of hours. It was a dream, a thrilling dream that someday surely would be realized.

"Yet without a way to stop our trains safely the future of railroading is lost to us," Towne concluded dismally.

George knew nothing about railroad brakes, though he had often seen the brakemen on the trains desperately whirling the handwheels to tighten the brakes before pulling into a station.

He asked the superintendent many questions about the braking systems in use, and in a few minutes found out more about railroading than he had known in all the years of his life.

Hand-braking was the only method known to slow down or stop a train. It was difficult and dangerous. Trains had to be limited to four or five cars. A brakeman stood between every two cars, and when the train reached a point about half a mile from where it was supposed to stop the engineer signaled "down brakes" by tooting the locomotive whistle. The brakeman began to turn a horizontal hand wheel that slowly tightened a chain forcing the brake shoes against the car wheels. When this chain was taut, he leaped across to the platform of the next car and performed the same operation over again.

Many of the brakemen were skilled at their jobs. Each tried his best to tighten the brakes exactly at the same time as the brakemen on the other cars so the train would be brought to a gradual, smooth halt. But no matter how expert they became, no two cars responded to the brakes at the same time. This caused them to bump into each other.

Freight trains were even harder to manage than passenger trains. On freights the handwheels were on top of the cars. The brakemen thus ran the risk of being knocked off by low-lying bridges, frozen in midwinter, or missing their footing on windy or slippery nights and hurtling down between the cars. Many brakemen lost their lives trying to perform their dangerous jobs.

Because of the primitive braking system the accident rate from collisions, derailings and other mishaps was fantastic. Almost every railroad line experienced several accidents a month. Inevitably they were traced to a failure to slow down or stop in time.

Very often, too, the brakemen would begin braking too late and the train would shoot past the station. It would then have to back in slowly, wasting precious time and holding up other trains.

All these difficulties wreaked havoc with time schedules

and inconvenienced passengers and freight shippers. As a result many travelers used the railroads only when absolutely necessary, while business concerns often preferred to ship by water because it was more reliable.

This then was the nature of the crisis facing the railroads as graphically outlined by Superintendent Towne. As George prepared to depart, Towne declared, "Westinghouse, someone once said it would take a thousand years to finish building the country west of the Mississippi River. But I tell you this—give the railroads a good brake, and we'll do it in twenty-five!"

All the way home to Schenectady George turned the superintendent's words over and over in his mind. Soon they began to repeat themselves in time with the clickety-clack rhythm of the train wheels.

Give the railroads a good brake, and we'll do it in twenty-five!

Each time the train slowed down to take a curve or stop to pick up passengers George was more aware than ever before of the bone-rattling jerks and starts and bumps that he had always taken for granted.

He recalled riding on a train once that had been held up for two hours because of a serious accident up ahead. Two freight trains had collided. When he saw them they were twisted masses of wreckage. One of the brakemen had been thrown off the top of a freight car and killed instantly, his broken body buried under a pile of shapeless metal.

George had been appalled at the tragedy but had accepted it as one of the hazards of life. Now, however, in light of what Superintendent Towne had told him he wondered why a better braking system couldn't be developed. Was it really an impossible task, or was it simply that no one had yet stumbled on the right principle? By the time the train reached Schenectady the following afternoon George's brain was whirling with ideas.

Marguerite met him at the door of his parents' house.

She was wearing a new dress and a radiant smile. George kissed her and said mischievously, "Are you confident your husband can invent anything he sets his mind to?"

"Anything," she retorted with a laugh. "I wouldn't put anything past you."

"In that case you're talking to the man who's going to revolutionize railroading!"

He told her about his discussion with Superintendent Towne. She listened attentively as he explained the need for a new type of brake that would help the railroad industry fulfill its true destiny.

"But do you think you can develop a better brake?" she asked. "After all I should imagine many men have put their minds to it unsuccessfully."

"I think so. Look at this." He took out a sheet of paper and swiftly sketched in a diagram showing a series of railroad cars.

"On the way home several ideas came to me," he explained enthusiastically. "One is to rig a braking device to the couplings that hold the cars together. When the engineer shuts off the steam the locomotive slows down. The other cars then tend to ride forward on their couplings. This pressure on the couplings would release a spring action forcing the brake shoes against the train wheels."

"But what advantage would that be?" Marguerite asked in a perplexed tone. "I'm afraid I don't have a head for such things at all."

"You see, darling, it enables the engineer himself to apply the brakes on all the cars at the same time," George went on patiently. "He doesn't have to depend on the brakemen to do it by hand. As things stand now, all he can do is signal 'down brakes,' and by the time the brakemen hear the whistle and respond, precious moments are wasted; moments that may make the difference between a safe stop or a serious accident."

Marguerite's face lit up and she said, "I think I understand it now. It's a very clever plan. But will it work?"

"I think so," George predicted confidently.

During the following month when he wasn't on the road he toiled away in his father's shop building a miniature train. The cars were held together by tiny couplings attached to a trigger device controlling the action of the brake shoes.

The miniature apparatus worked. But when George sat down to calculate the pressures needed to set the brake shoes he made a disappointing discovery. While the system was fine for a small train model it couldn't be applied to a real train weighing many tons and traveling at high speed. The tremendous force needed could not be controlled by a delicate trigger mechanism.

He ruefully discarded the idea.

Marguerite encouraged him to try again, though he needed no urging. Almost before he had given up on the coupling device, he paid a visit to the railroad yards, studied the cars and came up with an alternate plan. This idea utilized the chain principle already in operation. He would simply run a *single* chain underneath the full length of the train to the locomotive. Through a central control the engineer could draw taut the chain and clamp down all the brake shoes in a single motion. This would still have the virtue of his earlier plan, to eliminate the brakemen by enabling the engineer himself to apply instantaneous braking to all train wheels at the same time. The problem was to work out an efficient control device whereby the engineer could tighten the chain easily and quickly.

While George was pondering this puzzle he received a telegraph message from a Chicago customer. He was needed there to assist in preparing specifications for an important order. Although it meant being away from Marguerite he welcomed the chance to return to Chicago and see Superintendent Towne again, for he was anxious to get the railroad expert's opinion of his plan.

In Chicago he outlined the idea while Towne listened carefully and studied his sketches. "Now this is a curious coincidence," the superintendent said, scratching his head.

"We've been considering a chain design like yours for some months. It was submitted by a Milwaukee man. In fact, we've just completed outfitting our crack train, the *Aurora Accommodation,* with his experimental brake. The test run will be held tomorrow. Would you like to attend, Westinghouse?"

George was shaken. He had worked hard on his idea and it was a blow to find that someone had beaten him to it.

Towne evidently read the disappointment on his face, for he said, "Don't feel too badly. After all, we've been using chains all along so it's really not surprising that two of you came up with a similar adaptation at the same time. Now how about the trial runs tomorrow? Would you like to see them?"

George had planned to leave for Schenectady that afternoon, but the temptation to stay and watch the trials was strong, for he did not know when he would have another opportunity like it. So he said yes.

6

Harnessing the Wind

THE TESTS WERE TO BEGIN IN THE YARDS OF THE CHICAGO, Burlington and Quincy. George was introduced to the inventor, Augustine Ambler. They discussed Ambler's experimental system. It was amazingly like his own. It consisted of a long chain under the train running over a series of rollers connected to the brake levers of the different cars. The locomotive itself contained a bulky windlass and a complicated grooved wheel arrangement. The windlass was revolved by means of this wheel. It wound up the chain and by drawing it taut pressed the brake shoes against the wheels of the cars.

The windlass arrangement was a clumsy contraption with many complicated parts. George guessed it would not withstand much wear and tear. He was right. When the trial began, the brake not only failed to halt the train smoothly and quickly, but after the third stop the windlass device broke down.

As the train limped back into the yard George glanced at the crest-fallen face of the disappointed Ambler and felt sorry for him. Superintendent Towne was frowning as he wrote down the results in his report sheet.

No, a windlass would not work, George told himself. What was needed was a simpler device that could draw the chain taut with enough power to stop the train quickly.

Why not try steam? The thought popped into his mind

almost without conscious effort. Steam—of course! For him power and steam were by now almost synonymous. Hadn't it always proved to be the answer in the past?

Instead of a windlass why not substitute a steam cylinder underneath the locomotive and pipe in steam from the engine? The steam could then drive a piston which would be connected to the brake chain to draw it tight when desired.

When the disappointed Ambler had gone, George accompanied Towne back to his office and animatedly explained his idea.

"It might work at that," the superintendent said. "Certainly it's worth a try."

"If I work out the design, will you arrange to test it, Mr. Towne?"

The superintendent thought for a moment and said soberly, "I don't know. We invested a good deal of money to equip the train for today's trials. The brake was a failure. The directors of the road may not be willing to do it again."

George was disappointed, but he knew the superintendent was in no position to make a commitment without the approval of the board of directors. When he returned to Schenectady he told Marguerite he was determined to work on the brake even without a firm promise from the Chicago, Burlington and Quincy. "If the design is successful it will gain its own acceptance," he declared philosophically.

He started to refit the miniature train he had used earlier with a single chain and to rig up a tiny steam cylinder and piston. But even before he had completed the work he realized the principle was all wrong.

"You see," he explained to Marguerite, "the chain is fine provided the train is only four or five cars long. But suppose we want to lengthen it to fifteen or twenty cars? The chain would have to be correspondingly longer, and that would take so much power the steam cylinder would have to be larger than the locomotive itself."

"How do you know, George?"

"These calculations." He showed her a paper covered with

complicated equations for steam pressures and cylinder volumes and added, "No, I think I'm on the wrong track."

Marguerite stared unhappily at the sheet of paper and asked if he intended to give up work on the brake project. George studied her worried expression with an amused grin. "Of course not, darling," he said gently. "I'd hardly be worth my salt as an inventor if I gave up so easily. As a child I was so stubborn I would bang my head against the wall if I didn't get my way. Well, your husband is still determined to bang his head against a stone wall."

George revised the design. Instead of a single chain attached to a master piston in a huge cylinder under the locomotive, he decided to attach small individual cylinders under *each* car and to connect the cylinders to each other by pipes. All would then be fed with steam from the engine. The steam power would drive the individual pistons which would be attached to the brake shoes on the cars.

The job of refitting his model took weeks. Finally, it was completed. He fired up the tiny boiler. As the pressure rose he turned the valve that released the steam to the brake cylinders. Nothing happened. He increased the steam pressure. Still the system refused to work.

"I don't understand," he muttered. "It worked perfectly on paper."

In desperation he removed the cylinders and pipes piece by piece and tested the steam feed. The flaw was apparent at once. It was steam condensation that kept the brakes from working! Of course. What a dolt he'd been, he told himself. In his design he hadn't counted on the time it would take for the steam to travel from the locomotive to the individual car cylinders. As it passed through the pipes it condensed before reaching the rear cars. Thus there was no steam pressure to force the brake shoes against the wheels. Moreover, in the winter the condensed steam would probably freeze in the cylinders and pipes, creating an even greater problem.

George spent days trying to devise a way to eliminate the

temperature factor. But in the end he morosely decided that steam would not work.

Then a new problem rose to plague him. Sales of the frog and car replacer were not increasing as rapidly as his partners had expected. Rawls and Wall were impatient men who expected quick returns on their financial investment. George argued that it would take time to build up the business. He explained that since the equipment was made of cast steel it did not wear out as rapidly as the old cast-iron frogs. "But there are dozens of railroads throughout the country," he assured them. "They are all potential customers, once they hear about the durability of our equipment. The point is we must give ourselves time, gentlemen."

"The future doesn't interest me," Rawls replied irritably. "Wall and I have sunk a lot of money into this firm, and we mean to see a return on our investment. Not tomorrow but today!"

In spite of the mounting friction in the firm, George could not keep his mind off railroad brakes. Somehow, he would manage to solve the puzzle—of that he was as certain as his name was George Westinghouse.

It reached the point where every moment he could spare between sales trips was spent in his father's shop sketching designs or tinkering with his tiny trains. His mind was fired up with a dozen wild schemes, most of which he discarded before they were even down on paper. Those that did reach the drawing board soon disclosed some flaw which made them worthless.

One day at lunchtime George was at the shop munching a sandwich that Marguerite had packed for him that morning. His mind was a million miles away, searching for the missing link that would give him the answer he was seeking. Suddenly he was jolted back to earth by the trim figure of an attractive young lady coming up the walk. It was rare for a woman to visit the shop.

"What can I do for you?" George asked politely.

The girl, who was about nineteen, extended a magazine

called *Living Age*. She explained that she was selling subscriptions to earn her way through normal school where she was studying to be a teacher.

There was something about her that reminded George of Marguerite. So he took the copy and thumbed through it. Except for an article about the construction of a tunnel in Europe there was little in the magazine that interested him. But the hopeful look on the girl's face softened him, and finally he asked how much a subscription cost.

"Two dollars, sir," she said eagerly.

Mildly annoyed at his own weakness he reached into his pocket, took out the money and paid her. She carefully wrote down his name and address in her subscription pad.

George forgot about the incident until a few weeks later when the first copy of *Living Age* arrived. That evening after the family finished dinner, he and his father retired to the sitting room. His younger brother Herman went upstairs to study his lessons and Marguerite and Mrs. Westinghouse went to the kitchen to do the dishes. He picked up the magazine and turned to the table of contents. It was the same issue the young saleswoman had shown him. He flipped to the article that had first interested him and began to read.

The story was entitled "In the Mont Cenis Tunnel." It was a graphic description of the engineering difficulties encountered in boring a seven-mile-long hole through the Alps near the French-Italian border.

Tunneling through the mountain had been a monumental challenge. By normal engineering methods it would have taken fifty or sixty years! Instead, the engineers in charge of construction had tried to speed things up by introducing mechanized boring equipment, something never tried before. To power the machinery they had planned to use steam; but they found that the fire needed to manufacture the steam used up all the available air in the bowels of the mountain, leaving none for the workmen to breathe.

In the end the tunnel engineers had solved their problem in a revolutionary way—by using compressed air. They had

taken an air pump and hitched it up to a mechanized drill
which had been devised by an Englishman to operate on
steam power. The force of the compressed air drove the drill
like a battering ram against the face of the mountain and
punched through the rock in a fraction of the time needed
to do the job with pickaxe and human muscle. What's more,
the machine, instead of using up precious air, actually supplied it to the workmen inside the mountain!

As George read on a spark slowly kindled in his brain.

"The result," the article continued, "has been a perforat-
ing machine, moved by common air compressed to one sixth
its natural bulk, and consequently, when set free, exercising
an expansive force equal to six atmospheres. . . ."

George threw the magazine aside, fired with an inner excitement. *Compressed air.* In these two words he saw the dim
outlines of a monumental vision taking shape.

Scientists had known for a long time that air has bulk and
weight—that it was capable of exerting force. What, after all,
was the wind that turned windmills and drove sailing ships
but moving air? The scientists also knew that under normal
conditions air at sea level exerted a pressure of fourteen and
seven-tenths pounds per square inch. In scientific language
this was known as "one atmosphere." Physicists had evolved
a number of experiments to illustrate the power of air that
had been compressed to more than one atmosphere, but until
now little practical use had been made of this knowledge.

George saw at once that in compressed air, engineers now
had a source of power of fantastic promise. According to the
magazine article it had been sent through three thousand feet
of pipe and had retained enough force to batter a hole
through solid rock. Why couldn't it also be piped through the
length of a railroad train to force the brake shoes against the
wheels of the cars with enough pressure to bring the train
to a swift halt?

Unlike steam, there would be no condensation and conse-
quent loss of brake pressure. Nor would there be a need for

bulky windlasses or giant steam cylinders. No, air might prove to be the perfect answer. . . .

George's thoughts were racing along at top speed now. Almost from force of habit he took out a pencil and a used envelope from his pocket and began to draw. He sketched in a series of pipes. Let that be the tubes through which the compressed air would travel, he told himself. Between the cars he would connect the metal pipes by means of flexible couplings to prevent the pipes from bending or snapping when the train rounded a curve. The system would terminate at the locomotive where a simple air pump—similar to that used by the Mount Cenis engineers—would serve to compress the air. The pump would be driven by steam piped in from the locomotive engine. A valve device, operated by the engineer, would control the flow of compressed air through the system. Each car would have a small cylinder and piston device to force the brake shoes against the train wheels.

It was as simple as that.

So engrossed was George in what he was doing that he did not notice that Marguerite and his mother had come into the sitting room. He continued to study the sketch on the dog-eared envelope with wonder. Could it be that in less than half an hour he had solved the problem that had plagued railroad men for more than thirty years?

"George, what are you up to? You seem to be in another world."

Marguerite's voice brought him back to the Westinghouse sitting room. Mr. Westinghouse looked up from his newspaper and stared at his son while Mrs. Westinghouse smiled fondly and said, "I declare, George must be working on another one of his mechanical gadgets. He always has that faraway look when he's thinking his hardest."

George studied the faces of his wife and parents for a long, searching moment. He was so filled with the excitement of his discovery that he found it hard to know what to say.

Finally he swallowed and held up the sketch so everyone
could see.

"I think," he said quietly, "that I've found a way to stop
a railroad train."

No one said anything for a time. Then Marguerite broke
the silence. "That sounds wonderful, darling, but don't get
too enthusiastic. Remember, you were certain you'd solved
the problem before and then found out there was some
obstacle you hadn't foreseen."

"This time I *know* I'm on the right track," George replied
doggedly, out of some deep inner conviction of which even
he was not fully aware.

Mr. Westinghouse, who had been listening in silence, laid
aside his newspaper. "Well, you seem to be really sure of
yourself this time, George," he said. "What is it? Steam
again?"

"No, Father," George said. "Air."

"Air?" Mr. Westinghouse did not try to hide his astonishment.

"Yes, sir. Compressed air—something no one has thought
to use before. It's—well, it's like harnessing the wind."

He went on to explain the principle and showed Marguerite and his parents the magazine article, but his father stared
at the diagram on the envelope and shook his head skep-
tically. . . .

George spent a restless night, tossing so fitfully that Marguerite woke up to ask what was the matter. He whispered
that he couldn't sleep for thinking of his new idea. She suggested that a glass of warm milk might help.

He got up and went down to the kitchen and heated some
milk in a saucepan. After he drank it, he went to the sitting
room, lighted a lamp and sat down to read. He couldn't
concentrate on the printed page, his mind was so active, and
finally he laid the book aside and just stared at the lamp
and thought about his plans for the compressed air brake.
Just before dawn he managed to doze off.

He went to work at once preparing working drawings for

the new design. There were a host of mechanical problems to be ironed out and these he attacked with relish. The time he could devote to the brake was severely limited, of course, by his duties as chief salesman—indeed the only salesman—for Rawls, Wall and Westinghouse. Nevertheless, he managed to use his spare time so efficiently that within two months the drawings were completed and he was ready to begin thinking about constructing an experimental model. But in November, 1868, his work on the air brake was suddenly interrupted.

One afternoon he returned from a hurried trip to Albany to find an urgent message waiting for him from his two partners. "They want to see you at once," Marguerite told him. "Mr. Rawls says it is urgent. Is there trouble, George?"

"I don't know yet," he muttered. "They haven't made life easy for me these past six months, what with their constant complaints about poor profits."

When George showed up at the ramshackle foundry building that served as the firm's headquarters, Rawls and Wall were waiting. They looked grim. Rawls did the talking for the two investors. He informed George that because sales were not expanding at the rate they expected, they had decided a "business reorganization" was needed.

"But why?" George protested. "We're still showing a profit. A small profit, it's true, but you're not losing on your investment. A sound business venture needs time to expand. If you will only have patience—"

"We're tired of being patient," Rawls snapped. "Mr. Wall and I are businessmen. If we can't realize a quick profit, there's only one thing to do—sell our shares and get out!"

George was shocked by the sharpness in the man's voice. He asked warily, "What do you have in mind?"

"All right, I'll put our cards on the table," Rawls replied. "This business is not big enough for three partners. Either you buy us out or retire from the firm and turn the whole thing over to us." Wall, a pudgy little man who perspired a great deal, nodded nervously.

"Obviously I don't have the funds to buy you out," George said thoughtfully. "If I were to leave the business, what would you pay me for my patents?"

"Nothing."

George was astonished. "What do you mean, nothing?" he asked incredulously. "The replacer and frog are *my* inventions. Are you asking me to make you a gift of my patent rights?"

"We don't owe you a thing," Rawls insisted. "You've had the use of our money and have invested nothing except your time as a salesman—yet you've collected a third of the profits. What we intend to do is hire a salesman on a regular salary so we can lay him off when things are slow."

George's temper was mounting by the moment, the old uncontrollable temper that caused him so much trouble as a child when he felt he was being treated unfairly. However, through a supreme effort of will, he managed to hold himself in check. "I've also invested something valuable—my talent and skill," he retorted. "Doesn't that count for anything?"

"Talent, skill—nonsense, all of it," Rawls declared blandly. "It's money that counts."

George looked at the two older men and shook his head in a gesture of fury mingled with futility. "What kind of people are you anyway?" he asked. "Have you no sense of fairness or decency?"

"Business is business," Rawls replied.

"Yes," Wall echoed weakly. "Business is business."

"Well in that case we part company," George shot back. "But from this moment on you are not to use my patents without paying me a regular royalty. Do you understand?"

"We'll use them just as we have in the past," Rawls announced. "After all, Westinghouse, you *did* assign patent rights to the company."

"Yes, and once the company is dissolved you have no further rights to my inventions."

"We'll see," Rawls muttered. "A court of law may have something to say about that."

"I'd welcome a legal test," George replied curtly, before taking his leave.

Outside a howling wind bit through his clothing and chilled him to the bone. It had been an unhappy meeting. Apparently Rawls and Wall had planned to bluff him out of his share of the partnership but had not counted on his defiant attitude. Now they were left with nothing! It reminded him of the old fable about the man who killed the goose that laid the golden eggs.

Of course the experience had taught *him* valuable lessons, too. He had learned that success was not as easy as he'd assumed after making that first sale to Superintendent Towne. He smiled bitterly to himself. He had also found that in business there were unscrupulous persons who were only too eager to exploit others for their own gain. "May I never become so insensitive as to want to profit from another man's work without giving him his just share," he said half aloud.

As he neared the house he wondered how to break the news to Marguerite. It would not be easy to have to admit to his bride of a year that at twenty-two he was a failure, with no money or prospects for the future except a fantastic notion that he could use air to stop a railroad train.

7

The Air Brake Is Born

"MARGUERITE AND I HAVE DECIDED TO GO TO PITTSBURGH!"

This sudden declaration by George in early December of 1868 caught his parents by surprise. Marguerite, with whom he'd discussed the matter earlier, had agreed to let her young husband announce their decision.

"Why Pittsburgh?" Mrs. Westinghouse asked with a worried frown. "That's so far away—in the west of Pennsylvania."

George patiently explained that he had found a steel company—Anderson and Cook—which would make his frogs and replacers at a lower cost than the eastern mills. "They've agreed to cast the equipment at their own expense," he said. "And they want me to be their salesman. I'll be paid a royalty as well as a commission on each sale. Besides, there are many new railroad lines in that part of the country. They'll furnish a good market."

"But you can't take Marguerite to Pittsburgh," Mrs. Westinghouse protested. "You don't know a living soul there. Why you don't even have a place to live!"

"Marguerite and I have discussed that," George said. "If it's all right with you and Father, she'll remain here a while longer. Then, if things turn out well, I'll find a place and send for her."

Mrs. Westinghouse was somewhat relieved by this plan. "Why of course she'll stay here with us," she nodded assurance. "I still feel Pittsburgh is a far-off place, but I do think you're being sensible in not dragging Marguerite away before you know how things will go for you there."

Two weeks later George got off a train at Union Station in Pittsburgh, checked his two worn pieces of luggage with the stationmaster and set out in search of the steel firm of Anderson and Cook. It was located at the corner of Second Avenue and Try Street, but never having been in the city before he didn't have the foggiest notion of how to get there.

He stopped a passerby to ask the way. The stranger, a tall well-dressed young man, patiently gave him instructions for getting to his destination. George thanked him and was about to go when the man said, "Look, it's not a long way but the route is confusing if you're from out of town. I have a little time to spare. Come on, I'll take you there."

George protested that he didn't want to impose, but the young man insisted that it wasn't any trouble at all. So they started off.

When George said he was looking for the Anderson and Cook Company, his companion's face lit up. "I know the firm well," he replied. "I'm in the foundry business myself, you see. We do a lot of business with Anderson and Cook."

In a few minutes they were chatting away like old friends. The accommodating stranger's name was Ralph Baggaley. He was from a prominent Pittsburgh family and was employed as general manager of a local foundry. When they reached Second Avenue and Try Street, Baggaley gave George his card and invited him to visit his home some evening.

The meeting at Anderson and Cook went well. He spoke with Mr. Anderson, the senior partner, and confirmed the business arrangements they had agreed on in their exchange of letters. George was to start on the road at once drumming up trade from the railroad companies.

For the next two months he worked hard. He traveled almost constantly, staying in dingy hotels and skimping on meals to save money so he could send for Marguerite. He missed her terribly. On two occasions he almost wrote her to come even though he had barely enough money to cover her train fare, let alone rent a place to live. But in the end he knew they must be practical, so he simply wrote that things were going well, that he missed her and that he hoped soon to be able to send for her.

In the meantime he had not forgotten for a moment about his plans to build an air brake. He carried the drawings with him and whenever he called on an official of a railroad his sales plea for the reversible frogs and car replacers was inevitably accompanied by a discourse on the brake. Orders for the frog and replacer mounted steadily, but he could make no headway at all with the air brake. The chief obstacle was the expense. Like Towne in Chicago, most of the line superintendents recognized the need for a better brake, but they were unwilling to foot the cost of building an experimental set of brakes and making a train available for a test run. However, a few of the railroad men simply could not grasp the principle of using compressed air in spite of his attempts to explain it to them, and these dismissed it as a crackpot idea.

On one of his periodic stops at Anderson and Cook to pick up his mail there was a letter from the New York Central requesting him to come to New York City to give an estimate on an order. He was delighted. The New York Central, headed by Commodore Cornelius Vanderbilt, was one of the giants of railroading. A sale to this line would be large and mean a fat commission. Besides, what a wonderful opportunity to stimulate interest in his air brake! If any railroad was in a position to test the design it was the mighty Central with its huge array of up-to-date rolling stock.

It took three interviews with various members of the purchasing division to close the order for half a dozen pieces of equipment, but in the end the Central signed the contract. Flushed with success, George pulled out his air brake drawings and began to explain the idea to the purchasing executives, but they informed him they were not concerned with such matters. "This is a complex organization," he was told.

"The job of our division is to purchase routine equipment. You'll have to talk with one of the operations executives about your idea, Mr. Westinghouse."

George tried to get them to arrange for such a meeting but they refused. "We have nothing to do with that end of the business," they insisted. "Quite frankly we don't feel there's any point in our becoming involved in something that doesn't concern our division."

He thanked them and returned to his hotel. The satisfaction of having made the sale was somewhat dampened by his subsequent failure to work up interest in the air brake. Nevertheless, before going to bed that night he decided on a daring step.

He arose early the next morning and dressed carefully. After breakfast he took a hansom cab to the headquarters of Commodore Vanderbilt himself!

The head of the New York Central began his fabulous career by operating a ferry and still retained offices in the harbor district of Manhattan. For forty years he had climbed steadily, amassing steamship companies, building a railroad empire and acquiring important properties. Now, at the age of seventy-five, he was one of the most important tycoons in the world with a fortune estimated at $100,000,000.

George was received by one of the Commodore's secretaries, a patronizing, bespectacled young man with a sallow complexion. When George explained that he wanted an interview with the financier he was turned down brusquely.

"The Commodore sees no one unless he is referred here by someone the Commodore knows," the secretary declared haughtily.

"But I'm sure that what I have will be of interest and profit to him," George explained, patting the folder containing the air brake diagrams.

"Sorry, young man, but you cannot see the Commodore," retorted the secretary who was not much older than George.

"Very well, then I'll wait."

All morning George stubbornly waited in the reception

room hoping to catch a glimpse of the Commodore. By two in the afternoon he was half starved, but he wouldn't leave for fear of missing his quarry. Shortly before three o'clock there was a sudden flurry of excitement. Secretaries and clerks began to rush about busily. George sensed something was in the wind. Sure enough, a few minutes later a door opened and a large, florid-faced man wearing an expensive fur-collared coat strode through, followed by a small army of assistants.

George leaped to his feet and confronted the huge man. "Commodore Vanderbilt?" he inquired.

"Yes, yes. Who are you? What do you want?"

"My name is George Westinghouse, sir. I wonder if I might have an appointment—"

Two assistants rushed up to elbow the impertinent intruder out of the way, but George stood his ground.

"I never make appointments, young fellow," the Commodore declared. "I pay my secretaries to do that. See them."

"I did, sir. They tell me you won't see anyone unless—"

The Commodore was obviously in a hurry, and the unexpected interruption was a petty annoyance. But even Cornelius Vanderbilt couldn't easily brush out of his path a husky youth of over six feet who seemed determined to get what he had come after. The tycoon paused uncertainly. "Very well," he said at last. "John, take down this lad's name. I'll see him in the morning."

The next day George was back at ten. He waited for almost an hour. Shortly after eleven the sallow-faced secretary announced disdainfully that the Commodore would talk with him now.

George was ushered into a magnificent paneled office containing plush furniture and expensive Turkish rugs. The Commodore was seated behind a beautiful mahogany desk puffing a long, black cigar.

There were no preliminaries. "Well now, let's get to it," the railroad magnate said curtly without bothering to ask his visitor to sit down. "I have no time to waste."

George took out his drawings and went into a short, carefully rehearsed speech. He explained the principle of the air brake and used the drawings to illustrate it.

Afterward, the Commodore spat out a grain of tobacco, waved his hamlike hand at the sketches and retorted, "If I understand you, young fellow, you propose to stop a railroad train with wind. I'm too busy to listen to such nonsense. Good day."

That was the end of the interview. There was no opportunity to argue or plead for another hearing. The Commodore had rendered his verdict. George picked up his drawings and left.

The trip back to Pittsburgh was dismal. He had had his chance and failed. Perhaps there would not be another opportunity like it again. Only the thought that the commissions and royalties he had earned on the sale of the equipment would enable him to bring Marguerite to Pittsburgh kept him from being completely disheartened.

The next few days were busy ones. He managed to find two rooms at a clean but inexpensive rooming house in the city. He paid a month's rent in advance and moved in with his two pieces of ancient luggage. Then he sat down and wrote Marguerite a long letter giving her the good news about the sale to the New York Central and informing her that he had found a place to stay. He enclosed a draft to cover her railroad fare and other traveling expenses.

While waiting for his wife to arrive George filed a patent application for the air brake. He also wrote a letter containing a detailed description of the brake to Superintendent Towne to find out if the Chicago, Burlington and Quincy would be interested in testing it.

One evening, having nothing to do, he remembered Ralph Baggaley's invitation. After dinner he rode out to the Baggaley home. The young man welcomed him warmly and introduced him to his parents. For the rest of the evening they sat in the drawing room and talked. George told Ralph about his air brake and his unsuccessful meeting with Com-

modore Vanderbilt. Before the evening was over, young
Baggaley was almost as enthusiastic about the invention as
George himself.

"Why anyone would be so short-sighted as to overlook
such a marvelous idea is beyond me," Ralph said angrily.

"Money is a frequent cause of nearsightedness," George
observed wryly. "People are willing to listen, but when it
requires a cash investment their vision becomes blurred."

"What about your father?" Ralph suggested. "Can he lend
you enough to build a working model? Then you could take
it to the railroads and say, 'Here, I give you my new brake.
Test it.' "

"My father doesn't have that kind of cash on hand,"
George explained. "His funds are tied up in his shop. And
I'm already in debt to him for advancing me money to get
started with my car replacer. I wouldn't think of asking him
again. No, Ralph, this is something I've got to do on my
own."

The next day George rushed out to the railroad station
to meet Marguerite on the afternoon train. She stepped down
from the coach, looking prettier than ever. George caught
her in his arms, kissed her and whispered how much he had
missed her all these weeks.

She gave him the news from home. Rawls and Wall had
dissolved their partnership after an argument. They were
out of the railroad equipment business entirely, and he no
longer had to worry about them pirating his inventions.

"So the thieves fell out," he remarked. "Well I can't say
that I'm surprised."

Marguerite loved their little flat. She went to work at
once dusting, putting up new curtains and generally making
the place seem like a home.

One morning George got a letter from Towne. It was bad
news. The board of directors of the Chicago, Burlington
and Quincy had refused to authorize funds to construct and
test the air brake.

But the disappointment was short-lived. A few days later

George and Marguerite invited Ralph Baggaley to spend the evening at their home. After dinner Ralph puffed thoughtfully on a cigar and stared at the tiny fireplace where a log was crackling cheerily on the hearth. Finally he said, "George, I have a proposition for you. I have a few thousand dollars in the bank, and I want to invest in your air brake—"

George began to protest at once, but Baggaley declared, "No, no, before you say anything, please hear me out. With my investment you'll be able to build a complete brake system for a train. That way you'll be able to approach a railroad with something more than a design on paper."

"I won't accept your offer," George replied stubbornly. "It's too risky. Suppose I can't sell the idea to the railroads. You'll lose everything. No, I refuse to take advantage of a friend."

"Friendship isn't involved," Ralph replied with a laugh. "It's strictly a business arrangement. I come from a long line of shrewd Yankee traders, George. If I didn't feel it was a sound investment, I wouldn't have made the offer, I assure you."

George paused uncertainly. He turned to Marguerite and asked, "What do you think, darling?"

"The decision is yours to make," she said. "I believe in your idea, just as Ralph does. So I suppose that doesn't qualify me as an objective judge."

There was a long silence in the room. Then George said slowly, "All right, Ralph, I accept your generous offer. But I insist that we sign an agreement protecting your interest in the air brake."

Baggaley nodded with a grin. They shook hands to seal their partnership.

George got to work immediately arranging for the construction of a braking system. Through Ralph's connections they managed to have the job done almost at cost at Atwood and McCaffrey, a local firm. The completed mechanism, though built from the detailed working drawings, followed almost exactly the original diagram George had sketched on the back of the dog-eared envelope months before. It consisted of a steam-driven pump that compressed air into a main reservoir and maintained it at a constant pressure of sixty or seventy pounds per square inch. A pipe from the reservoir led to a valve mechanism that served as the engineer's control and to a line of three-quarter-inch pipe that ran the length of the entire train. This "main pipe" was actually a series of pipes connected between cars by three-ply rubber hose. Under each car quarter-inch "elbows" connected the main pipe to a cylinder and piston which in turn were connected to the brake shoes.

To stop the train the engineer would simply open the valve to let compressed air from the reservoir rush into the main pipe and then to the car cylinders. To release the brakes the compressed air was simply discharged into the atmosphere through the engineer's valve.

George had added one new feature to his original design. He had devised a simple valve arrangement to be fitted to the flexible hose couplings between the cars. When the two parts of a coupling were joined, the valve opened, and when they were separated the valve automatically was pulled shut by a strong spring. Thus if a car were separated from the rest of the train after the brakes were set, compressed air could not escape and the brakes on both the detached car and the train itself would continue to be effective. This was especially important to prevent equipment from rolling downhill when it was parked on a grade.

The design was so simple it took only a few weeks to construct, although George could only spare time in between sales trips to supervise the work of the mechanics. When the brake system was completed, he brought Ralph into the shop and showed it to him. "And we still have money left over," he announced enthusiastically as he pulled out an itemized list of expenditures and handed it to his partner.

With Ralph's help George succeeded in getting an interview with an official of the important Pennsylvania Railroad. The executive examined the brake equipment and was impressed. "I intend to present the matter to our board of directors," he promised faithfully. But that was the last they heard of it. As the weeks passed they received no word from the Pennsylvania, and they could only conclude the railroad had lost interest.

One morning George was seated at the desk provided for him at Anderson and Cook poring over his monthly accounts when a husky, middle-aged man came into the office.

"Where can I find Mr. Westinghouse?" he inquired.

"I'm George Westinghouse."

"You?" The stranger seemed incredulous. "I—well frankly I'd expected to find someone older."

"Oh, I'm Westinghouse, all right," George said with a grin.

"W. W. Card is my name," the visitor announced. "I'm the superintendent of the Panhandle Railroad. I'll come right to the point, Mr. Westinghouse. Some of my friends at the Pennsylvania Railroad tell me you've put together an unusual brake. I want to know more about it."

George pulled out the working drawings and spent the next ten minutes explaining the principle. Superintendent Card studied the diagram carefully. Then he said, "It sounds good. If this air brake of yours does all it promises to do on paper, you'll have revolutionized railroading. Why we can cut running time in half. Where can I inspect the equipment?"

George dropped everything and took the superintendent down to Atwood and McCaffrey where the apparatus was stored. Card examined each piece, asked numerous questions, then said, "Well, I'm impressed, Mr. Westinghouse. I'd like to bring the purchasing agent of our road here to look at it, too."

Two days later Card returned with the purchasing agent who went over the braking system and agreed to submit a recommendation to the board of directors of the Panhandle.

After the disappointing experience with the Pennsylvania, George and Ralph fully expected the matter to drag out for weeks. This time, however, things happened at breakneck speed. Exactly a week later Superintendent Card was back with a proposition.

"My road has agreed to authorize a trial of your equipment," he declared. "We'll make the *Steubenville Accommodation* available to you—it's a locomotive and four cars. The run will be out of Pittsburgh. But you'll have to install the air brake at your own expense and guarantee to reimburse the Panhandle for any damage. What do you say, gentlemen?"

George and Ralph stared at each other incredulously. This was the chance they had been waiting for! They could hardly believe their ears.

"We're happy to accept your offer," George told Card quickly. "I'll get to work at once having the brake installed so we can hold the trials as soon as possible."

Later the two young partners realized that the expense of installation, when added to the earlier cost of building the sample braking system, entailed a far greater expenditure than they had anticipated, but they were so overjoyed at the prospect of a real trial that they did not even stop to wonder if they had acted rashly. Furthermore, they estimated if they cut labor costs to the bone by helping out with the mechanical work themselves, they could get by on the money left over from Ralph's original investment.

Their calculations turned out to be almost too close for comfort. When the installation job was completed, Baggaley counted up their funds and discovered they had less than ten dollars in cash!

On a crisp morning in April, 1869, George kissed Marguerite good-bye and went out to Union Station where he met Ralph. The *Steubenville Accommodation* was waiting in the railroad yard. Her engine was already fired up and her stack hissed black smoke. While they awaited the arrival of Superintendent Card and the other Panhandle officials, George made a last-minute check of the brake components. The system was in perfect order. When the superintendent's party arrived, Ralph joined it and they all got into one of

the passenger cars while George climbed aboard the locomotive behind engineer Daniel Tate.

"Okay, Dan, let her go!" he said.

Tate clanged his bell, released the brake valve and slowly
opened the throttle. With a reluctant creak the train began
to move. It crept slowly through the yard and chugged its
way out onto the open Steubenville track. Tate explained
to George that in a few minutes they would come to the
Grant Hill tunnel. George nodded and whistled happily to
himself.

Suddenly, as he gazed out at the gleaming rails he froze.
Several hundred yards ahead, at a surface crossing, a wagon
drawn by two horses was parked squarely across the train's
path! A terrified drayman was lashing at the horses' flanks.
All of a sudden the frightened horses broke sideways and
hurled the driver off his wagon and onto the track.

George glanced frantically at Tate. He could tell by the
engineer's face that he had seen the entire incident. Tate
cursed aloud and reached for the brake valve, turning it all
the way. There was a loud grating sound as the pistons
under the cars drove the brake shoes against the wheels with
tremendous force. The train ground to a halt so suddenly
that George was almost thrown off his feet. The locomotive's cowcatcher had stopped little more than a yard from
where the drayman lay on the tracks paralyzed with fear!

From the rear of the train there were shouts from Superintendent Card and the other officials who came running
to find out what had happened. White-faced at the thought
of the tragedy that had been averted, George explained
everything while Tate and the fireman helped the drayman
to his feet. Fortunately the driver had suffered only minor
bruises.

The superintendent slapped George on the back and
congratulated him. "Well your brake is a success!" he declared flatly. "It's proven itself beyond question." The other
Panhandle officials agreed.

However, George insisted that they go through with the

trial as planned. Card shrugged but instructed Tate to continue the run.

The rest of the trial was an anticlimax. The engineer tested the brakes a dozen times under varied conditions. He set them at slow speeds and at high speeds, on curves and on steep grades.

The mechanism behaved faultlessly.

When the train returned to Union Station George and Ralph rushed to the tiny flat to tell Marguerite the good news. She kissed George happily and ordered them to get ready for lunch even though they protested that they were too excited to eat.

Three months later, in July, 1869, George and Ralph met with Superintendent Card and a group of leading railroad men in the Pittsburgh area. All had seen the air brake in operation and were enthusiastic about it. By formal vote they agreed to organize a corporation to be known as the Westinghouse Air Brake Company, with a capitalization of half a million dollars.

Ralph told them that the firm with which he was associated was going out of business and explained that its foundry could be converted into a plant to manufacture the air brake. Everyone approved the idea.

Next came the election of officers. Ralph Baggaley was among those named to the board of directors. Then, on motion by Superintendent Card, the group unanimously named twenty-three-year-old George Westinghouse as president of the new company.

8

Revolution in Railroading

THE AMERICA OF 1869, THE YEAR IN WHICH THE WESTING-
house air brake was introduced, would have been unrecog-
nizable to the founding fathers. The agrarian nation of
Washington, Jefferson and Benjamin Franklin was on the
threshold of a new industrial age whose pace had been
quickened by the frenetic industrial demands of the Civil
War. In farming and manufacturing, in science and discovery, a revolution was already under way, with significant
consequences in human thought and outlook.

While industrial change was taking place in the countries
of Europe as well, it was in the United States that it proceeded at its most rapid, dramatic rate. Here it was accompanied by a mood of soaring confidence and burgeoning
vigor. Whereas in times past new inventions and important
discoveries were often greeted by public apathy if not resentment, suspicion or fear, a different attitude now seemed to
prevail among the American people. Mesmerized by the
miraculous changes that had already been brought about by
such inventions as the telegraph, steam engine and photog-
raphy, the public was willing to look, listen and be amazed
by anything new.

It was in this era of self-confident eagerness and wide-eyed
receptivity to change that George Westinghouse introduced
his new air brake. Curiously sensitive to the current mood
of the American public, he decided from the start that his

91

first task must be to demonstrate to the man in the street what his brake could do. "My idea," he told the Board of Directors of the Westinghouse Air Brake Company, "is to outfit an exhibition train and give public demonstrations in the large cities."

"But it's the railroads we want to convince," one of his colleagues protested. "Why bother with the public at all? Shouldn't our efforts be restricted to selling the road executives on the merits of the brake?"

George replied, "No. From personal experience I know how conservative the railroads can be. On the other hand if we win the people—the train-riding public—to our side, *they* will do the job of convincing the railroads far more effectively than we could ever hope to do."

After some discussion the directors approved George's plan. He contracted at once to have a train fitted out with a set of air brakes, and he demonstrated a shrewd sense of salesmanship by selecting railroad cars that were plushly upholstered and up-to-date, for he wanted the brake to be associated in the public mind with the most modern achievements in railroading.

With George aboard and in charge of all arrangements, the train chugged to Philadelphia, Chicago, Indianapolis, St. Louis and Milwaukee in the late fall of 1869. At each stop it was boarded by newspapermen, mayors, governors and key railroad officials, who were then taken on a trial run while George explained the air brake's safety and financial advantages, pointing out that it would help speed up railroad transportation and improve the comforts of train travel, thus attracting many new customers.

The tour was superbly successful. In each city visited, great crowds of people turned out to watch the demonstration. Reporters wrote lengthy articles about the remarkable new air brake, and editors filled their columns with lyrical praise of the device and its inventor. Pictures of George appeared on the front pages of newspapers throughout the country. In some of the smaller towns the local bands turned out to greet the demonstration train, for many communities along the railroad lines soon realized the transportation revolution created by air braking would mean a major expansion of business and community life.

Requests began to pour in from other cities and towns to have the train brought to their localities. Happily George agreed to expand the itinerary. What had started out as a brief demonstration trip to a few major cities turned out to be an extended tour of the entire East and Midwest.

Soon orders came in from railroad purchasing agents all over the country for braking equipment. They flowed in so fast that the factory in Pittsburgh could not keep up with them. The plant was enlarged. Even so letters had to be sent out apologizing for manufacturing delays. Moreover, as the first pieces of equipment were received and tested in day-to-day operations, the railroads were so enthusiastic they immediately reordered in large quantities, thereby intensifying the production bottleneck.

In spite of the favorable reaction of many of the road executives, complete victory was not achieved overnight. At the start it was mostly the smaller roads who were eager to install the air brake. As rivals of the giant lines, they saw in George's invention a way to improve their position. By stressing safety and speed they could now compete more favorably. The big railroads, on the other hand, had tremendous sums invested in existing braking equipment and did not want to junk it in favor of the air brake, even though the latter made the contemporary brakes entirely outmoded.

In addition, the manufacturers of hand-braking equipment were not eager to be put out of business by a twenty-three-year-old upstart. So they joined forces with some of the railroad giants to ridicule the Westinghouse invention. They took out advertisements and started rumors in an attempt to depict George as a charlatan and his air brake as untrustworthy. Among the stubborn opponents was Commodore Vanderbilt, who still refused to concede that a train could be "stopped by wind."

In spite of these organized efforts, public opinion grew in George's favor. Anyone who traveled on a train equipped with air brakes saw its advantages at once. Public demands to force the giants to install Westinghouse brakes grew, but a few, like the Commodore's New York Central, continued to hold out.

Then on a freezing night in February, 1871, the Central's crack *Pacific Express* chugged out of New York City on its way to Chicago. The *Pacific Express* was Commodore Vanderbilt's personal pride. He boasted of it as "America's Number One Train" and insisted that his personal friends use it when traveling to and from Chicago.

Shortly before ten o'clock the *Express* approached a bridge over Wappinger's Creek seven miles below Poughkeepsie, New York. A few minutes earlier a southbound train, consisting of twenty-five tank cars filled with oil, had snapped an axle on a forward car and jumped the tracks. The tank cars had piled up on the bridge.

As the *Pacific Express* rounded a bend the bridge hove into view. The horrified engineer saw the derailed freight train and frantically signaled for "down brakes." But it was too late. The crack flyer ploughed into the tank cars.

The locomotive plunged from the tracks into the icy waters of Wappinger's Creek, dragging the baggage and express cars with it. Five sleeping cars and a day coach remained on the bridge and were shrouded in flames within a few seconds. The bridge, now a fiery mass, collapsed and hurtled into the blackness below.

In all, thirty persons were killed and scores injured in the tragedy. It was described as one of the worst in the history of railroading. Public demands for greater railroad safety were now so overpowering, even the Commodore could no longer resist them. In the face of the *Pacific Express* disaster his last-ditch opposition to air brakes collapsed, and the New York Central placed an initial order with the Westinghouse company. Within a few years all of its passenger trains were equipped with air brakes.

General acceptance of the Westinghouse system set in motion a far-flung transportation revolution. The air brake was now being hailed as the most important safety device ever developed. Since the end of the Civil War the railroad industry had been expanding steadily. Now it burgeoned at a fantastic rate. Superintendent Towne's earlier prediction that an efficient brake would speed up railroad development was thoroughly validated. Accidents fell off to a fraction of the former rate. Train speeds and schedules were stepped up as traffic boomed. All over the land new trackage began to appear, tying towns and cities together with sinews of gleaming steel.

Ralph Baggaley, Superintendent Card and other officials of the Westinghouse Air Brake Company were delighted with the booming market. Ralph told George, "If the demand continues at the present rate we'll have to expand facilities again. We're more than a month behind in orders as it is."

In spite of the multitude of administrative tasks which his role as president demanded, George spent every spare minute in a makeshift shop he set up at the air brake factory. Many times, when the regular working day was over and the employees went home, he put on a pair of soiled overalls and continued to tinker at a workbench long after dark. Being a perfectionist he felt there was still room for improvement in the brake. He modified the valves, couplings, air pump and other parts of the system so often Ralph said in mock exasperation, "When the mechanics come in in the morning they lay wagers as to what modifications will be made that day!"

What was actually driving George was not change for the sake of change at all, but rather a desire to make his invention as nearly foolproof as possible. While he knew the air brake was the safest, most efficient ever devised, he was also aware that equipment, no matter how carefully manufactured, could break down through constant use, abuse or human error.

George more than anyone else felt a strong sense of responsibility for the consequences of his invention. He knew that before the air brake, trains were forced to travel at slow speeds because there was no way to stop quickly in an emergency, and now engineers could open the throttle, secure in the knowledge that they had good brakes under them.

What if the air brake were to fail on a train going at top speed? he asked himself over and over again. The result would be a monumental tragedy that could conceivably dwarf even the *Pacific Express* disaster. He was convinced that the only answer was to justify the engineer's faith in the brake by making the equipment so perfect that it could not break down under any circumstances. Yet he also knew that from a practical standpoint this was impossible. Brakes were made by human beings. They were made of steel. Human beings could err. Steel could twist or break under stress.

So George went to work adding more modifications to help diminish the possibility of mechanical breakdown. He changed valve designs, added reinforced parts, substituted improved steel. Even after numerous changes were made he was still dissatisfied.

Taking a coldly analytical approach, he decided to tackle the problem from a new direction. Suppose he redesigned the mechanism so that it would be applied *automatically* if there was a mechanical failure? While studying the problem George did not take anyone into his confidence for he knew how hard it would be to explain that he intended to build an air brake that would work when it did not work. It was a paradox that no person in his right mind would accept. Yet the pages of history were filled with discoveries that had proceeded from concepts that had seemed bizarre at the outset.

One afternoon while tinkering with a model of an air brake, a simple idea occurred to him. What if air pressure were used not to apply the brake shoes but to release them? In the standard or "straight" air brake which they were now manufacturing, the shoes were forced against the wheels of the cars by increasing pressure, and when air was discharged from the braking system into the atmosphere the brakes were released from the wheels.

George stared dumbly at the model. It was so simple, so beautiful, so perfect even he was astounded. He analyzed the problem from the beginning, to make certain he had not overlooked anything. The chief danger in the present design, he knew, stemmed from the possibility of leakage developing in the system. If the steel piping cracked or was ruptured by collision or if the rubber hosing between the cars suddenly tore or sprung a leak, compressed air would rush out and the engineer would have no pressure with which to apply his brakes. He would be absolutely helpless.

However, if he were to reverse the entire scheme and compressed air in the main brake pipe were to be used to continually *keep* the shoes from bearing on the wheels, the danger would be eliminated entirely. To stop the train the engineer would simply decrease the air pressure in the system. If hose or piping were to rupture and a leak developed, it would be the same as if the engineer had lowered the air pressure. The brake shoes would be forced against the wheels automatically and the train would be brought to a safe, immediate stop until the brakes could be repaired. What's more, if a car became uncoupled from a train while the train was in motion, the same thing would happen—the brakes on that particular car would apply themselves automatically!

Once George had hit on the theory, the mechanical details were surprisingly simple to work out. After a week of trial and error he came to the conclusion that the simplest approach was to mount individual reservoirs of compressed air under each car, and these small storage tanks of air would be connected with the main reservoir and air pump in the engine. It would be these individual compressed air tanks under the cars that would actually do the work of applying the brake shoes. For this new system he designed a new valve. When the compressed air pressure in the main brake pipe was lowered by the engineer or by a mechanical mishap, a "window" in the valve—which would be placed between the car reservoir and the brake cylinder—would be opened and the brake shoes would be clamped against the wheels automatically, actuated by the compressed air in that particular car's storage tank.

When the new brake went on the market in 1874 it replaced the old straight air brake almost overnight. George's reputation was firmly established by now, and the railroads were willing to accept the automatic brake almost exclusively on his say-so. This time there were few of the doubts and hesitation that preceded full acceptance of the earlier version.

Meanwhile the patents credited to him were beginning to pile up at an amazing rate. The new features for the automatic brake alone resulted in a patent a month. Nor did he stop trying to perfect it. In spite of its already excellent performance he continued to introduce improvements regularly.

The demand for air brake equipment was now growing overseas, too. In the next few years George visited Europe several times, and as a result, affiliate companies were started in England, France and Russia.

In addition, he was gaining a widespread reputation for his enlightened employment practices. One of his major accomplishments at this time was the introduction of a "piece work" system to enable his men to earn more money.

"Look," he told his employees, "the more money you earn the more money the company makes. Therefore, I am willing to pay you on the amount of work you do rather than on a straight wage basis."

The result was a flock of applications for employment at the Westinghouse Air Brake Company, for the mechanics found they could earn an average of four dollars a day with George, whereas in other shops two dollars and fifty cents a day was considered an excellent wage.

From his own early experience as a shopworker, George

knew that the better the tools the better the product, so he saw to it that his shops were equipped with up-to-date machines. He inaugurated the custom of holding an annual dinner for the workers at the Union Station Hotel in Pittsburgh, and every Thanksgiving he presented turkeys to all of his employees.

When other company heads complained that he was spoiling his men and thus making things difficult for them, he retorted sharply, "I'm not stopping you from doing the same thing. In the Westinghouse Company I want the men to feel they're working with me, not for me. Treat your men right and they'll treat you right!"

During the Westinghouse Company's embryo years, George and Marguerite continued to live simply in a modest rented flat. In 1876 he decided to surprise her. It was the year of the famous Centennial Exposition in Philadelphia, commemorating the hundredth anniversary of the Declaration of Independence. Visitors came from all over the world to view the exhibits which demonstrated the latest discoveries in science and industry. As a gesture of appreciation to his employees, George chartered a special train to take them to the World's Fair for a week's expense-paid holiday.

It was a thrilling experience. Among the most spectacular displays was the railroad exhibit which contained a model of the Westinghouse air brake. But there were other interesting inventions, too, including a new device called "the telephone" built by young Alexander Graham Bell and apparatus to improve telegraphy by a virtually unknown inventor named Thomas Alva Edison.

One morning soon after their return to Pittsburgh George suggested to his wife that they take a pleasant ride to the suburbs. He hitched up the carriage and trotted the chestnut mare to a lovely section at the eastern edge of Pittsburgh, known as Homewood. Wheeling sharply, he drove into a graveled driveway lined with great shade trees. A beautiful, three-storied white stone house came into view, surrounded by a spacious velvety lawn.

The sight left Marguerite breathless. "It's gorgeous," she exclaimed. Then she added quickly, "Are we allowed here? This is private property and I'm afraid we're trespassing."

"I think not," he said matter of factly. "It's ours, Marguerite, if you want it. I took an option on it as a birthday present for you."

Marguerite's eyes widened, and she said timidly, "Oh George, do you think we can afford it?"

"It's our first real home," he replied tenderly. "You've waited a long time for it, dear. So I think you're entitled to it no matter what the cost."

They drove on in silence. Then Marguerite said, "I have a name for it."

"For what?"

"Our new home. I want to call it *Solitude*."

9

The Busy Years

IN HIS THIRTIES NOW, GEORGE HAD CHANGED. IT WAS AS IF worldly success, which had come to him so early in life, had sobered and matured him. On the surface at least he was no longer the high-strung temperamental youth given to flying off the handle when things did not go as he wished. By now he had learned to keep his ungovernable temper in check at all times. At first it had called for a supreme effort of will, but he managed to win out over himself. No small part of it was Marguerite's doing, for she had convinced him that in dealing with other businessmen he could not wear his temper on his sleeve.

The battle within himself had been so difficult, however, that in the end he went almost to the other extreme. To those who did not know him well he appeared stolid— phlegmatic almost—because he seemed slow to anger and slow to show enthusiasm. But to those who knew him and understood him, the surface stolidity was merely a protective mask. In the intimacy of family gatherings and parties for his close friends he was still the idealistic, sensitive George Westinghouse of his youth, quick to show hurt or anger in the face of cruelty or thoughtlessness in others.

However, in physical appearance the changes were more apparent. By the time he was thirty his hair had turned prematurely gray, and he had put on considerable weight. So much so that Marguerite was constantly pleading with

101

him to watch his diet. The fleshiness made him appear much older than his actual age, which at times proved to be an advantage, since most of his business dealings were with men twice his years.

By 1878 life for the Westinghouses had settled down to an active but satisfying routine. The startling beauty of Marguerite's early youth had softened into the more mature radiance of womanhood, and George was never prouder than when he could show her off to his friends and business associates. Though most of their time was spent at Solitude, they visited George's parents in Schenectady frequently. Mr. Westinghouse was still actively engaged in business, and when his famous son came to town he delighted in bringing him to the shop, proudly introducing him to the new men with the boast that "George got his start in this very shop in spite of me!"

George's brothers were also doing well in their particular fields. The eldest, Jay, was a successful businessman, while John was engaged in social work. All three Westinghouse girls were married and raising families. Herman, the youngest child, though still in school, showed such a talent for engineering that George promised to find a place for him in the Westinghouse Company after he completed his education.

In spite of the company's startling growth, George was still not satisfied that he had perfected his brake to the ultimate point. While the automatic air brake had successfully solved the safety problem, he felt there was still room to improve the brake's efficiency. For example, while it was now standard equipment on passenger trains it had never made headway in the freight field. As late as 1880 brakemen were still employed to climb on top of freight cars and apply the brakes by the ancient handwheel method. The reason was a simple one. Passenger trains were limited to a maximum of half a dozen cars, but the growing demand for overland transportation of goods necessitated that freight trains become longer and longer. Indeed unless a single

engine and crew were employed to transport twenty or
twenty-five cars, freight rates could not be kept down to a
reasonable level. In some cases a single train contained as
many as thirty or forty cars.

While the Westinghouse air brake worked beautifully
for the shorter passenger trains, compressed air power could
not be transmitted swiftly enough to bring a huge freight
train to a smooth halt. True, if the engineer applied the air
brakes in an emergency it would bring the cars immediately
behind the locomotive to a sudden jarring stop, but it took
many seconds for the "serial action" to reach the last car.
As a result, these rear cars would smash into the halted cars
in front and smash fragile freight shipments and injure
cargoes of livestock. Moreover, many trainmen were hurt
during emergency stops, which was an experience not unlike
a collision with a stone wall.

When George made up his mind to tackle the problem of
freight-train braking, some of his associates tried to convince him to stick to the field he knew best: air brakes for
passenger trains. "We've got the finest brake in the world
for passenger trains," they pointed out. "Why it stops them
so fast that its own efficiency is the thing that hinders it for
freight work."

Nevertheless, George went ahead with experiments to
make a version of the air brake that could be used effectively
on freight trains. Ever since the Centennial Exposition, when
his eyes had been opened to the limitless possibilities of
electricity by the early inventions of Bell and Edison, he
had been intrigued by the potential use of this new source
of power for railroading. In a wild moment he asked himself
why, if electricity could be used to send telegraph signals
or even the human voice over wires, it could not be utilized
to operate the air brake on a train. If he could hook up an
electrical circuit from the engineer's control handle to the
compressed air valves under each of the cars, the actuating
of the brake shoes on the rear cars would no longer depend
on the relatively slow passage of compressed air power

throughout the length of the train. Each valve would respond instantaneously to the engineer's control, thus bringing every car in even the longest freight train to a stop at the same split second. Electricity would serve as the trigger, while compressed air would do the heavy work!

He rigged up a model circuit and connected it to the air brake system. It worked, but sporadically. Unfortunately he had not counted on the ease with which wires snapped and electrical connections came apart under the grueling wear and tear of railroading. In the end he decided electricity was too erratic to be trusted to control an air brake where safety was all-important. No, he would have to try some other approach.

So he began at the beginning again. Taking a standard set of automatic air brakes he pulled it apart piece by piece, studying each part carefully. He modified the valve system to speed up the serial action and designed a new "triple valve" to be installed on each car. It increased the efficiency perceptibly. Finally he hit on the idea of enlarging the diameter of the compressed air pipes themselves to enable power to be transmitted faster.

When these modifications were completed, George had a fifty-car train fitted with the improved model at a cost of two hundred thousand dollars. Even Ralph Baggaley, as secretary of the Westinghouse Air Brake Company, was skeptical of the wisdom of expending that amount of money. When George asked him and the other directors to come along on a trial run, Ralph shrugged and observed, "Very well, since it is probably the most expensive ride in the history of railroading."

George insisted that his associates ride in the very last car to test for shocks and jars, but before the huge train chugged out of the yard he did something that amazed Ralph and the others. He set up a glass of water on the floor of the car.

"Keep your eye on that glass," he instructed the party.

As the train picked up speed all eyes were glued on the tumbler.

George stood poised, with his watch in his hand. Suddenly a trainman stationed in the car called out, "The engineer has applied his brakes, Mr. Westinghouse. I just received the signal."

Swiftly, smoothly the huge train came to a complete stop.

"Two and a half seconds!" George shouted triumphantly. "It took only two and a half seconds to bring this train to a halt."

Ralph pointed to the glass on the floor and observed excitedly, "Why there wasn't enough jar to upset that tumbler of water!"

The party climbed out of the train and George instructed the engineer to repeat the test while he and his associates watched from the side of the tracks. The engineer backed off slowly toward the railroad yards and made his run again, applying his brakes at a prearranged point. When the train came to a halt, George directed an assistant to measure the distance. To the amazement of everyone the brakes had brought the train to a stop from a speed of twenty miles an hour in less than two hundred feet.

Superintendent Card, who had been a railroad man for thirty years, shook his head in amazement. "I never thought anything like this would happen in my lifetime," he declared in a tone approaching reverence.

The perfecting of the Westinghouse air brake had revolutionized railroading. It made it possible to increase speeds with complete safety to forty, fifty and even sixty miles an hour, so that in many cases running time between terminals was cut in half. In the single decade between 1870 and 1880 the accident rate was slashed so dramatically that the American public lost its fear of traveling by train. Now, with the utilization of the air brake for freight work as well, a new era in transportation was born in the United States. To meet the demands imposed by the new popularity of railroad travel the roads were forced to step up their schedules by adding more and more trains between terminal points. Thus a new dimension was added to the technical demands made on those who ran America's railroads—traffic control.

Because of his close association with the railroad industry George was well aware of the burdensome problem of regulating traffic, though at first he had no intention of involving himself in a field he knew little about. But his resolve did not last long. Innately curious, he wondered why trains which could make a run, say, from Pittsburgh to New York in record time under good traffic conditions, frequently lost as much as five or six hours because of tie-ups and traffic snarls at intermediate points. He knew that controlling trains on the line as well as scheduling was an administrative problem, yet he couldn't help wondering if better controlling devices could not make the job easier. Moreover, the utter confusion that seemed to pervade railroad traffic control by 1880 had increased once more the hazard of collision and other serious accidents.

Investigating the problem with his usual thoroughness and attention to detail George found that in one important area of traffic control—traffic signaling—the United States was still at a primitive stage, with England far ahead in this field. True, a few of the leading American roads had gone to the expense of installing the English system, known as "block signaling," at some of their busier railroad yards, junctions and crossings; but the vast majority of trackage throughout the nation was entirely unprotected.

The purpose of signaling was to reduce accidents and keep traffic moving with frequency, regularity and at given speeds. Under the block system a track was divided into sections, or blocks, ranging from half a mile to four miles in length. At the junction of two blocks a signal station was set up in charge of a signalman who raised a "danger" signal when a train approached and kept it up until the signalman at the station ahead telegraphed an "all clear" for the block. Then the first signalman flashed the train engineer to go ahead. This system was hazardous—the signalman might fall asleep or be taken ill or flash the wrong signal by mistake.

By the time George finished his study of the English block system he had carefully listed the drawbacks as well as the advantages. He also familiarized himself with experiments by British railroad experts with an innovation called "interlocking," a system whereby huge levers controlling the railroad switches and signals in a block were assembled into a single machine and interlocked with each other, so conflicting signals could not be given. It was a vast improvement, for it meant that even if a signalman were blindfolded and pulled levers at random, he could stop traffic and produce confusion, but a collision would not result.

George realized at once that while block signals combined with interlocking meant increased safety, it still did not fulfill the need for a more efficient system of signaling. Just the moving of switch and signal levers by hand took such physical effort that only a muscular man could manage it. Why not use mechanical power? he asked himself. Why not compressed air? Air pressure was powerful enough to exert the tremendous force needed to bring a fifty-car train running at maximum speed to a full stop in a few hundred feet, so it certainly could be harnessed to do the work of a man, even a muscular individual.

Quietly but methodically he set to work designing a series of signals that could be operated by a simple air valve. The basic principle was identical with that of the air brake, but instead of forcing a brake shoe against a wheel the new devices would be geared to open and close track switches and raise and lower signals.

Almost at once he ran into the problem of controlling the compressed-air devices. At first he had planned to have the air pump and compressed-air reservoir in the signal station itself, with long underground lines carrying the air pressure to the switches and signals. The flow of compressed air would be controlled by the signalman, who would simply turn a valve handle similar to an engineer's brake handle on a

locomotive when he wanted to throw a switch or raise a
signal. But as George got more deeply involved in the project
he realized that it would never do, for the expense of installing compressed air lines for hundreds of feet would be
prohibitive. What's more, if one of the air lines ruptured
or sprung even a small leak, the entire line would have to be
dug up to detect and repair it. No, it would not do, he told
himself, for if the system was to be practical at all it would
have to be simple, relatively inexpensive to install and easy
to maintain.

Reviewing his experience with the air brake, George recalled his unsuccessful experiments with electrical circuits
to control the compressed-air valves on trains. Because of the
wear and tear on the wires and electrical connections result-
ing from the jarring movement of the train he had ruled out
the use of electricity for braking controls. But in the case of
switches and signals the danger of broken circuits and torn
wires was greatly decreased, for there would be no stress and
strain to contend with. If an air pump and reservoir could
be installed close to the switch or signal, and an electrical
circuit hooked up between the compressed-air equipment
and the signal station, the system could be operated by
remote control. By simply throwing a switch the signalman
would send electrical current flowing through a wire to
activate an air valve near the track. It was that simple. There
would be no lengthy air lines to install and maintain, no
need to worry about elaborate, expensive repair jobs. Even
if the compressed-air equipment or the electrical circuit
were to break down, the trouble could be detected and
repaired in a fraction of the time required to overhaul an
all-compressed-air system.

Once he had ironed out the theory George found that the
actual designing of what he referred to as his "electro-pneumatic system" was simply a matter of practical experimentation to work out the details. As the work progressed additional ideas occurred to him, such as the principle of using

the metal rails themselves to carry the electrical current. This had a twofold advantage, for not only did it cut down on the amount of wiring required but it served as an automatic safety feature. If a switch were opened by accident or a piece of track were broken, the electrical circuit would be interrupted. George used this principle to devise an automatic danger signal that would be raised by compressed-air power the moment such an occurrence took place. He also applied this concept to design a simple apparatus that would automatically set the air brakes on a train if the engineer happened to pass a danger signal by mistake.

By the end of autumn of 1880 George had succeeded in completing blueprints and working models for a dozen signals, switches and other traffic control devices operating on the electro-pneumatic principle. His first reaction was to call in Ralph Baggaley, Superintendent Card and his other associates in the air brake company and convince them to invest in his new inventions, but he soon had second thoughts on the matter. During informal discussions with several railroad officials he knew well, he discovered to his dismay that they were not at all enthusiastic at the idea of spending their roads' money on "elaborate frills" such as automatic signals. Even when George showed them the models of his inventions they shook their heads and declared that the railroad industry was not ready to invest in such advanced systems. They left him with the clear impression that for the moment it was enough for them that the railroad industry was booming and the profits were rolling in, so why tamper with good fortune?

Though George had long ceased being amazed at the myopic vision of many of his fellow industrialists and businessmen, he asked himself testily why it was that so many of them couldn't see farther than their noses until it was almost too late to do anything about it. Nevertheless, recognizing the reality of the situation he was faced with, he decided it would be unfair to let his associates assume the financial risk of investing in the manufacture of the equipment with almost no possibility of gain. No, if a risk had to be taken he would take it personally, he decided.

He explained the situation to Marguerite and confessed frankly that they would be venturing most of their private funds on what might well prove to be a losing proposition. "Does it mean a great deal to you, George?" Marguerite asked.

"A great deal," he admitted.

"Will it mean giving up Solitude?"

George smiled. "No," he said. "I think we can manage without taking a chance on losing our home."

Early in 1881 George announced the organization of a separate corporation—the Union Switch and Signal Company—to manufacture and install electro-pneumatic railroad equipment. As he had anticipated, initial growth was slow, but in spite of this discouraging start he began to wage an unremitting campaign to convince the railroads of the advantages of his new traffic control devices.

Fortunately for the new company his efforts were not a total failure. A few roads did submit orders for equipment and installation, largely on the basis of his personal reputation as the pioneer of the Westinghouse air brake. When these early systems were put into use the immediate reaction of the railroad officials who had shown the foresight to invest in them was one of enthusiasm. While this helped convince a few, it took years before the signaling devices gained the full acceptance that the air brake had achieved. Among the few heartening signs was a letter from the superintendent of a small independent Pennsylvania railroad, one of the first lines to order and test a Union Switch and Signal system. The superintendent ended his letter this way: "If the men who work the railroads ever choose a patron saint it will be St. George—in honor of George Westinghouse."

10

Energy from the Earth

IN THE SUMMER OF 1883 MARGUERITE ANNOUNCED SHE WAS going to have a baby.

For George it was a crowning experience to learn he was to become a father. Now thirty-seven, he was one of the nation's most successful young industrialists. He had wealth, fame and the satisfaction of doing the work he loved most —inventing. His and Marguerite's life together was idyllic and by all accounts they could want for nothing more. While they were deeply appreciative for all the good things that had happened, they felt that in one respect life had cheated them, for they were still childless after sixteen years of marriage. They had just about given up hope, when the family physician confirmed the fact that Marguerite was pregnant.

So it was not surprising that the news rather stunned George. Usually calm and unruffled under fire, he became a typically anxious father-to-be. Marguerite tried to reassure him by pointing out that birth was the most natural occurrence in the world. "Why babies have been born since the beginning of time," she said with a laugh.

But his anxiety was not abated that easily. He was convinced she should seek the services of a specialist, for he couldn't help wondering about her failure to have a child all these years. "Nature is wise beyond our knowledge," he told her. "She must have had a sound reason for not seeing fit to bless us earlier. Why should we take a chance now?"

They took the problem to their physician who pointed out that he had no reason to believe the birth would not be normal. "Nevertheless," he conceded, "you may be right, Mr. Westinghouse. There are many things we doctors do not pretend to know."

Since there were few specialists in Pittsburgh, the doctor referred them to a distinguished practitioner in New York City, and in early winter they took a train east and settled in a suite of rooms in one of New York's best hotels.

At George's insistence Marguerite visited the specialist regularly. Shortly after New Year's she was admitted to the hospital to have her baby. To George's great relief the birth was perfectly normal. "Mr. Westinghouse," the physician announced approaching George who was pacing restlessly back and forth in the waiting room, "you are the father of a healthy boy." George felt the tears well up in his eyes, and he tried to thank the doctor, but no words came.

They named the baby George.

New York was experiencing a good deal of sub-zero weather that winter, and the streets were almost constantly covered with snow, so on the advice of the physician they decided to remain in the city until the baby was at least a month old. With time on his hands George tried to keep busy. While Marguerite nursed the baby or shopped in the fine New York stores, he held conferences with his eastern representatives and attended to other business matters. Mr. and Mrs. Westinghouse came down from Schenectady to see their brand new grandson. They brought Herman with them, and George decided that the young man should go to Pittsburgh to work in the Union Switch and Signal Company where he could learn practical engineering from the ground up.

In spite of his attempts to keep busy, George was restless. He longed to get back to productive work in Pittsburgh, and he grumbled to Marguerite about it. She chided him for refusing to accept their prolonged stay as a rare opportunity to enjoy a vacation and observed that it was he who had insisted that they come to New York in the first place. "Now that we are here," she added, "let's pretend we are on an extended holiday."

George shrugged and told himself that women simply did not understand the problems of men. He might have minded his inactivity less if he could spend time with his son, but he was permitted in only at specified intervals by the grim-faced, middle-aged hired nurse. She even dictated to Marguerite in no uncertain terms.

To while away the time he had the Pittsburgh newspapers delivered every day and read through them for every scrap of local news. It was in one of these papers that he came across an account of the commercial development of natural gas deposits in a suburb of Pittsburgh known as Murrysville.

George read the story with great interest, for gas had been a subject of wide public attention in the last few years. As a fuel its properties had long been known, and in recent decades it had begun to see widespread use for home lighting. Made from coal and transported in special tanks, it burned cleanly and was a great improvement over the oil lamps of an earlier era.

However, in 1879—just four years earlier—Thomas Alva Edison, the brilliant young inventor whose work had first been acclaimed at the Centennial Exposition, announced a remarkable achievement—the invention of an incandescent electric light. With this single accomplishment Edison had sounded the death knell of the gaslight era and sent the stocks of gas companies tumbling.

Some farsighted engineers maintained that even if the electric bulb did eventually replace the gas jet for lighting, the real potential of gas had not yet been tapped. They felt it could surely be used as a fuel for cooking, heating and in industry. But such speculation was purely theoretical, since everyone knew that to manufacture and transport coal gas in the quantities required for such purposes was entirely out of the question. In reply, the gas experts contended that if natural gas, which came from wells, could be discovered close to the industrial and residential centers where it was to be used it might prove to be an ideal substitute for the more expensive coal gas.

It was with these considerations in mind that George read about the discovery of natural gas only twenty miles from Pittsburgh and found himself speculating wildly about the prospects it held out. Suppose the engineers were right, he told himself—suppose natural gas could be found in sufficient quantities to serve consumer needs—why, in time it could be used in millions of homes and in thousands of factories that now depended on coal as a primary fuel. The possibilities were almost endless, he was convinced.

Although George knew next to nothing about geology, he visited the library in New York City and began to read whatever sparse information was available on the subject. He learned that the discovery of gas or oil deposits in one locality was usually a sign that it was also present in the general area having the same geological background. This led to even wider speculation, and he began to wonder if natural gas deposits were not a phenomenon of the whole Pittsburgh area, not just Murrysville. Once his powerful imagination took wing, it began to soar and he even convinced himself that underneath Solitude itself might be just such a source of gaseous fuel.

When he, Marguerite and the baby returned to Pittsburgh in March, one of his first acts was to visit the natural gas wells at Murrysville and learn all he could about drilling from the field engineers in charge. Finally he took one young supervisor aside and offered him a generous fee to come out to Solitude on his day off and examine the land there.

The following Sunday the engineer showed up and spent the afternoon walking around the estate, swooping up occasional fistfuls of earth which he smelled, tasted delicately with the tip of his tongue and rubbed gently between his fingertips.

His verdict was a cautious one. "There might be natural gas here," he told George. "That's always a possibility, for the soil composition is somewhat similar to Murrysville, and we know the geological makeup of the whole area is related. But to be perfectly frank, the only sure way to tell is to drill a test hole."

George asked him how much it would cost. He frowned and thoughtfully estimated that such a project might run to five thousand dollars.

That evening George discussed the idea with Marguerite, and although she did not share his enthusiasm at the prospect of having a noisy pumping machine chug-chugging on the lawn all day long, she finally consented provided there would be no drilling within a hundred yards of the house itself.

The following week George hired a drilling crew and on the advice of the foreman chose a spot behind the stable as the most likely place to sink the hole. For the next three weeks there was a constant din at Solitude as the giant drill, driven by its noisy engine day and night, bit deeper and deeper into the ground.

Each evening after returning from the city, George gulped down his dinner hurriedly and like a small eager boy got into his dirty overalls and went outside to watch the drilling operation. Some of his friends and neighbors joined him, so that soon it became a sort of nightly ritual.

When the drill worked its way down to more than fifteen hundred feet there were only faint signs of gas. George couldn't help feeling discouraged. One night he went to bed wondering if it wouldn't be wiser to call the whole thing off before he sank more money into the useless hole in the ground.

Shortly before dawn he and Marguerite were rocked out of a sound sleep by an earth-shattering roar. George sat upright in bed.

"What is it?" Marguerite asked in a frightened whisper.

"An explosion of some sort," he said. "Do you hear that?"

"What?"

"That steady roaring sound," he replied.

"The baby!" Marguerite cried, jumping out of bed. "He may be in danger!"

"I'm sure there's no danger," he tried to reassure her, though he was very puzzled. "The noise isn't near the house. It seems to be coming from the stable—"

— Suddenly he pounded his huge fist into the palm of his hand and shouted excitedly, "The gas well! It must have come in!"

He threw on a pair of trousers and a jacket and raced out of the house. In the pinkish pre-dawn glow he saw a startling sight. The area behind the stable looked like the aftermath of battle. It was an indescribable mixture of sand, gravel, mud and dirty water. The top of the drilling derrick had disappeared—apparently blown off by the explosion—and the drilling apparatus itself was buried beneath a mass of rubble.

The night drilling crew were cheering excitedly, and the foreman ran over to George and pumped his hand. "It's the bonanza of gas wells, sir!" he shouted. "I've drilled many a hole but I've never run across anything like this! Look at that pressure, Mr. Westinghouse!"

It was indeed something to see. The water, sand and mud, propelled by the force of the natural gas, formed a geyser a hundred feet high.

Soon the fountain subsided and was transformed into a stream of pure gas.

"How do you plan to cap the well?" George asked the foreman.

The man tugged at his ear thoughtfully and said, "I don't rightly know, sir. Never been faced by pressure this great before."

Nevertheless, he ordered his men to place a heavy spruce plank over the hole as a temporary measure. They dragged the plank into position and tried to drop it over the well opening. At that precise moment it was caught in the jet of gas and propelled straight up into the air like a straw in a gale. It smashed into one of the iron beams of the derrick with such force that the wood split into a dozen pieces.

The workmen then tried to lower a hundred-pound stone

into the hole, but the pressure merely lifted the rock and balanced it in midair like a balloon.

They decided to give up for the time being, and George went back to the house to tell Marguerite the exciting news.

The next day they succeeded in capping the well with special equipment brought in from the city. But now there was the problem of how to control the flow of gas inasmuch as it was under such tremendous pressure. George discussed the matter with the head foreman but he was told there was no satisfactory method. "That's the trouble with natural gas," the foreman added. "It's uncontrollable, unpredictable. People are afraid to play around with it. The dangerous pressure makes it almost impossible to pipe safely."

"Don't worry," George told him. "We'll find a way."

He got to work at once at his drawing board, and that evening showed his sketches to the foreman. "My idea is to install a stopcock arrangement at the well opening," he said. "It will serve the same purpose as a water tap. Can you have this made up at once?"

The foreman studied the diagrams and nodded. "It's simple enough to have made, Mr. Westinghouse. No reason why it shouldn't work, either. But what about piping the gas from the well? That's the real problem."

"I have an idea or two on that too," George replied. "For the time being though, let's concentrate on controlling the gas at the source."

Within a week the stopcock apparatus was in place and could be turned on or off at will. George also had the crew install a sixty-foot-long pipe straight up in the air to tap off the gas so it could be tested for its illuminating and burning properties.

He invited some of his friends and neighbors to the show. At a given signal one of the drilling crew attached a small bundle of oily rags to a primitive pulley arrangement, touched a match to it and pulled it up by means of a rope. Someone turned on the stopcock to let gas into the pipe and when the burning rags reached the mouth of the pipe it ignited a pillar of fire a hundred feet high. The giant torch pointed toward the sky like a fiery finger and illuminated the area so brightly it was possible to read a newspaper by its light more than a mile away!

Now that he had proven a point George was faced with the problem of what to do with his gas well. His original intention had been to find out whether natural gas existed in or around Pittsburgh. He had informed Marguerite that if natural gas were found he would have it piped into the house for their personal use. "Perhaps if there's enough," he had ventured, "we'll even be able to supply some to our friends in the neighborhood."

However, now that the drilling had brought up a "gusher" new vistas had opened up. George couldn't help speculating that with several wells of that size there would be enough gas to supply the entire city of Pittsburgh and the surrounding area.

He discovered that one large manufacturing concern in the city was already using natural gas, but the expense was enormous, for every cubic foot of gas had to be piped more than twenty miles from Murrysville. He was convinced that with a huge supply closer at hand, it would be possible to reduce the cost so much that gas would eventually replace coal in popularity for home and industrial use in Pittsburgh.

The first step, George decided, was to form a company to dispense the gas. The next problem—how to distribute it—was not so simple, for as the drilling foreman had indicated earlier, the piping of natural gas under high pressure was hazardous. If he were to transport it into the consumer's home or factory through underground mains—like the city's water supply—he would have to get the permission of the Pittsburgh City Council to install pipes under the streets, and this would be impossible unless he devised a safe method. Because of its tremendous pressure the gas forced itself through every minute crevice in the transporting pipes so there was a constant danger of accidents. Seeping through the ground the gas would find its way into a home or other closed area, and the stage would be set for a disastrous explosion. One recent tragedy had created such a commotion that there was talk of outlawing the use of natural gas altogether. A hostler had gone into a stable one evening and struck a match to light a lantern. The next thing he knew there was a tremendous explosion that wrecked the building, killed a valuable mare and hurled the man himself more than thirty feet through the air. Although he had escaped with his life the incident had dramatized the perils of natural gas, for an investigation disclosed evidence of nearby gas seepage.

Once the dimensions of the problem were clarified in his own mind, George approached it analytically, and his earlier experience working with steam and compressed air under high pressure stood him in good stead.

Even as a youngster in his father's shop he had learned that every steam engine was provided with an "escape valve" to prevent the buildup of dangerous steam pressure. Later, this principle—the release of high pressure through a valve arrangement—had been used in his design of the air brake. So it was natural that he should turn once more to the escape valve concept in connection with natural gas.

Suppose he were to install valves at designated points along a gas pipeline, valves that were constructed to open at a given pressure? He had already designed such a mechanism for the air brake, and it would be simple enough to adapt the idea to the present problem, he told himself. In that way the gas would be under control at all times, and where it did build up to unsafe pressure it would escape at safe, predetermined points, not through dangerous underground seepage.

He now extended his thinking a step further and asked himself what drawbacks there would be to such a system. The first that occurred had to do with the possibility of a malfunctioning of the valve arrangement. With natural gas coming out of the ground at pressures high enough to smash steel drilling equipment, what guarantee was there that it would not blow out a delicate, precision mechanism like an escape valve. This was a danger that had to be taken into account, no matter how strongly constructed the system itself was.

The answer, George felt, lay in providing a double safeguard, so that even if something went wrong the hazard would be minimized until repairs could be made. He searched around his cluttered workroom and spotted two small lengths of metal pipe of different diameters. It gave him an idea. Suppose the natural gas were to be transported in a small gauge pipe which, in turn, was enclosed in an outer "protective" pipe? he asked himself. He fitted one of the pipes into the other and studied it carefully. If the double-pipe arrangement were extended throughout the entire system, gas that escaped at the joints of the inner pipe because of the high pressure would be trapped in the outer pipe, he reasoned. *But it would be contained at a much lower pressure than in the actual transport pipe and would only gradually build up to a dangerously high pressure.* Now if he were to attach escape valves at certain points along the outer pipe, they could be set to open at a much lower pressure than he had originally planned, thus providing a double, virtually absolute safeguard against accidents from gas escaping at high pressure.

By the time he completed his blueprints for the gas control system, his application for permission to lay gas mains under the city streets was already before the Pittsburgh City Council. When word of his plan spread the reaction was instantaneous and violent. Many citizens, whose fears were inflamed by the press accounts of recent explosions, protested that the plan was dangerous. Others claimed it was unfair to grant Westinghouse a virtual monopoly in the distribution of natural gas. The distributors of coal and other competitive fuels encouraged the controversy. They took out newspaper advertisements attacking George's plan and reminding the public of the perils of natural gas. They even hinted that Pittsburgh was in danger of total destruction if an explosion should take place under the city streets.

George defended his project by issuing detailed statements to the press outlining the safety precautions he had devised. As a gesture of good faith he even offered to furnish the city's fire houses and police stations with fuel gas without charge.

"I have no ambition to hold sole control of natural gas," he argued. "Nor do I have any intention of making exorbitant profits or dictating to any business or manufacturing interest. What I am seeking is a way to distribute the benefits of my discovery, receiving only a fair compensation for my property—nothing more."

After three weeks of public debate George added an even more generous proposal. He volunteered to use his pipeline to transport and distribute the gas of any other producer at a nominal charge, the charge to be set by mutual agreement or by an impartial arbitration committee.

Unable to turn down such an inviting proposal, the City Council finally voted him permission to install the underground pipes.

Meanwhile he continued to improve his designs for the transporting system and gas escape valves. He also perfected a gas meter and improved well-drilling apparatus. Before he was done he had thirty-eight patents for discoveries in the natural gas field alone!

On August 4, 1884, an advertisement appeared in local newspapers announcing the formation of a company to supply and distribute natural gas to the citizens and industrial concerns of Pittsburgh. It was to be called the Philadelphia Company, and the president was to be George Westinghouse.

In a short time the new firm became the principal supplier of fuel to the city and the surrounding area. As word spread of the availability of an ample and inexpensive supply of natural gas in Pittsburgh, the producers of heavy metals who needed massive quantities of fuel began to weigh the advantages of establishing their mills there.

Within a few years Pittsburgh came to be known as the steel and iron capital of the United States.

11

Magic from Wires

WHILE GEORGE WAS BUSY DEVELOPING HIS NATURAL GAS SYS-
tem, Thomas Alva Edison, whose invention of the electric
light had initially threatened to ruin the gas industry altogether, was faced with a serious dilemma. His incandescent
bulb, now five years old, had made far less of an impact
than had been expected. In 1879, when Edison first announced his achievement, editorial writers had glowingly
prophesized that the tiny glass globe would have revolutionary results, but these predictions had failed to material-
ize. In truth, electric lighting was still a novelty, and the
vast majority of homes still retained the old reliable gas jet
which had served so well in the past.

The trouble lay not with the incandescent light itself but
with the difficulty of transmitting current to power the lamp.
In order to supply electricity, power stations had to be set
up every few thousand feet, and the heavy copper cables
required for transmission made the cost prohibitive for every-
day use, and retarded its development.

George, who had followed Tom Edison's meteoric career
with avid professional interest, although he had never met
him personally, was well aware of the difficulties that beset
his fellow inventor and sympathized with him. Moreover,
as a result of his work on electro-pneumatic railroad switches
and signals, his interest in electricity had been whetted and
he began to read everything he could lay his hands on that

concerned itself with this remarkable new source of power.

Shortly after completing his successful development of the natural gas system, George received a pamphlet from Great Britain that told about a remarkable invention by a Frenchman named Gaulard and an Englishman named Gibbs. The device was called a "secondary generator" or "transformer." From the very moment that he finished reading the account, George was convinced that he had stumbled onto the mechanism that would ultimately revolutionize the field of electricity.

In its earliest beginnings, electricity had been produced by batteries which created a small, steady current that flowed in one direction only and was known as "direct current." All early motors and other electrical devices were designed to operate on direct current.

However, with the development of the dynamo which was driven by steam or water power and produced large quantities of electricity, a new type of current was created. It was produced *not* by chemical action, as in a battery, but by *magnetic* action, for a dynamo was simply coils of wire whirling around in a magnetic field. This new type of current flowed first in one direction, then in the other, and was known as "alternating current."

In order to utilize alternating current for motors and other direct current equipment, the "commutator" was developed. It was simply a device to convert alternating current from a dynamo into a flow of direct current.

Unfortunately direct current had a serious disadvantage because it was a "high current" traveling at a "low voltage." Voltage was the "pressure" that "pushed" electricity along a conductor. In their laboratories physicists had discovered that a high voltage could send a low current over a line much more efficiently than a low voltage transmitting a high current. The latter required thick, costly copper wire as a conductor, for a lot of electrical energy was converted to heat and wasted. Thus it could not be sent more than a few hundred yards without becoming prohibitively expensive, and generating stations had to be set up at close intervals to supply power.

So costly was direct current that it loomed as the major stumbling block to further electrical development.

It was no wonder then that with his lifelong habit of poking his curious nose into everything, George Westinghouse found himself fascinated by the Gaulard-Gibbs transformer. The published account described it as a simple device made up of two coils of wire separated from each other. When an alternating current was sent through one of the coils it "induced" a current in the other. And, depending on the number of turns of wire in each coil, the transformer had the amazing ability of "stepping up" or "stepping down" voltages. Thus a voltage sent through a primary coil having ten windings would induce in a secondary coil having a hundred windings, a voltage ten times as great. At the same time, the size of the current would be decreased to one-tenth. By simply reversing the coils a voltage could be stepped down in the same way, and the amount of current increased.

George was aware from the pamphlet's account of the Gaulard-Gibbs transformer that it was still in a primitive state, that it was little more than an experimental curiosity, but it was enough to spark his imagination. He was soon convinced that the invention held the key to the whole problem of electrical development, for if voltages could be stepped up a hundred, even a thousand times or more, it would be possible to use inexpensive small-gauge wire to transmit electricity over vast distances. In this way the cost of power would be low enough to benefit communities everywhere.

There would be problems, of course, and one of the most important was how to utilize high-voltage current safely. It was well known that such current could cause serious injury, even death, and if his idea was to succeed, adequate safeguards would have to be devised. The solution, he decided, was to install a transformer to step up the voltage at the source of power for efficient, inexpensive transmission over well-insulated lines, then reversing the procedure at the receiving end by using another transformer to step down the voltage to a safe level for use in the home or in industry.

A second problem stemmed from the fact that while the transformer worked only when alternating current was used, electric motors were all designed to operate on direct current. It was for this reason that commutators were installed on dynamos generating electricity—to change the alternating current produced, into direct current that could be used. Here again his analysis of the difficulty led to a solution that was startlingly simple—he would eliminate the commutator from the source of power, the dynamo, and place it at the point of use, in the motor itself. In this way alternating current produced at a power station would be stepped up in voltage for transmission, stepped down again at a receiving station and converted into direct current only after it reached the motor.

Explaining the idea to his brother Herman who was now fully involved in the Westinghouse enterprises, he announced that he was prepared to go into alternating current development on a major scale. "I want you to coordinate the program," he said. "The first step is to send a man to Europe to buy the American patent rights to the Gaulard-Gibbs device, and I don't want him to come back without it!"

A young engineer, Guido Pantaleoni, got the assignment. Less than a month later he cabled from England that he had tracked down the inventors and closed the deal. The price was fifty thousand dollars.

Pantaleoni returned, bringing with him a signed agreement and several sample transformers. When George examined them he was astonished at their appearance, for they were crude devices made of stamped copper disks and soldered joints. "Why these look like laboratory toys, and poorly made ones at that," he observed with dismay. "They aren't nearly ready for commercial development."

Herman asked if they had erred in purchasing the rights

to the transformer so hastily—sight unseen, in fact—and George replied that they would soon find out. He directed an engineer to hook up one of the devices to an electrical circuit, and he and Herman watched carefully while tests were carried out.

In spite of its primitive appearance the transformer worked, but George knew at once that it would never do from a practical standpoint because to produce it in quantity would involve an endless job of hand-soldering and fitting copper disks into place. The expense would be prohibitive, he pointed out.

During the next few days he applied himself conscientiously to improving the Gaulard-Gibbs design, but after making several changes he realized that the basic construction concept itself was faulty. Scientifically, the transformer principle was sound, but mechanically the device was completely wrong. So he decided on a drastic step: he would discard the Gaulard-Gibbs transformer and start from scratch using the same principle but make an entirely new design of his own!

The principal task was to discover a quick, inexpensive way of winding the primary and secondary coils, and here he decided to return to that remarkable all-purpose machine he had learned to use as a boy—the lathe. Instead of complicated copper disks and soldered joints, why not wind the core with ordinary insulated copper wire? he asked himself. Taking a laminated iron core, he locked it into the jaws of a lathe, wound a few turns of wire onto the machine and started it. As the lathe spun he played out more wire. It reeled itself onto the core neatly in a matter of seconds. Why it wasn't so different from the old trick of using a lathe to cut iron pipe, he told himself with a grin as he recalled that first summer in his father's shop.

Since voltage was stepped up by the same ratio as the windings on the transformer's primary and secondary coils, the lathe proved to be perfect for the job. Winding a thousand or two thousand turns of wire onto the core was now

no task at all. Within three weeks George had designed a
new transformer that bore almost no resemblance to the
Gaulard-Gibbs apparatus. His engineers suggested other improvements, and these, too, were incorporated into the Westinghouse design.

On December 23, 1885, George, his brother Herman and
a group of associates applied for a charter to establish a new
corporation for electrical development, to be known as the
Westinghouse Electric Company.

The charter was granted and George lost no time in getting started. He had recently moved the Union Switch and
Signal Company to a suburb of Pittsburgh, and since the
old factory was standing idle, he put it to use manufacturing
electrical equipment.

One of his key men was a young engineer, William Stanley,
who had contributed valuable suggestions for improving the
Westinghouse transformer. Just as they were about to begin
commercial development, Stanley came down with a pul-
monary ailment and announced he was returning to Great
Barrington, Massachusetts, where his parents lived.

"I'm sorry to let you down, chief," he told George apologetically.

"You're not going to let me down," George replied. "You
didn't think I was going to allow you to get away from me,
did you? Here at Westinghouse we consider talent a valuable
asset." He told the surprised engineer that he was assuming
the entire expense of setting up a special laboratory at Great
Barrington where Stanley could prepare a practical demonstration of the transformer's use in the transmission of alternating current. He also promised to assign another engineer named Belfield to go to Massachusetts to assist him
in the project.

For the next three months Stanley and Belfield worked
entirely on their own. George gave orders that any equipment they needed was to be shipped from Pittsburgh at
once. When Stanley sent an urgent message asking for a
special type of dynamo one of the men in the supply division

of the Westinghouse Electric Company came running to George's office frantically waving the request.

"It's from Stanley, sir!" he exclaimed. "Now he wants a new kind of dynamo."

"Well send it to him," George replied without looking up from his drawing board.

"But he's beyond his budget," the exasperated employee protested.

"Send it to him anyway," George repeated as he held up a sketch and examined it critically.

"But you don't understand, Mister Westinghouse. This dynamo can only be obtained from England. It will have to be shipped at enormous expense."

George put down his drawing, winked in a conspiratorial manner and said, "Let's order the dynamo anyway, Sanders. It will be *our* secret, yours and mine. And if you promise not to say anything about Stanley's budget, I'll not say anything about it, either."

Sanders left wearing a perplexed frown.

In mid-March of 1886 George received a telegraph message from William Stanley. It read, "All is ready. Come at once."

George dropped everything, and he and Herman—who served as vice-president of the Westinghouse Electric Company—boarded a train for Massachusetts. In Great Barrington they were met by Belfield who took them out to Stanley's laboratory.

Stanley, a thin pale man with intense features, showed them around the small building. George and Herman were amazed at what the two engineers had accomplished in such a short time. They had set up a full-scale generating plant using the dynamo imported from England. They had also installed a power line from the dynamo to a building in the town of Lawrenceville, four miles away. Using transformers, they had stepped up the voltage at the dynamo to three thousand volts for transmission.

George, Herman, Stanley and Belfield climbed into a

carriage and drove to Lawrenceville, leaving a technician in charge of the dynamo. When they arrived at the town they followed Stanley into an old building where a dozen Westinghouse transformers piped off electricity from the power line and stepped down the power to five hundred volts. The current fed four hundred incandescent lamps which had been installed around the building.

"Have you tried it yet?" George asked, examining the system with his meticulous eye for detail.

"No, chief. We wanted you to have the honor of pulling the switch the first time," Stanley said, his bony face relaxing in a smile.

"How do you know it will work?" George shot back with mock severity. "You didn't drag me out here on a wild goose chase, did you?"

"Well we did 'cheat' a little," Stanley admitted. "A few weeks back we installed a system like this in Great Barrington. We wired a couple of stores for lighting. But the lamps were only a short distance from the dynamo."

"Did it work?"

"Beautifully."

"Very well, let's get on with the show," George said.

Without further ado he turned on the master switch. Four hundred lamps sparked to life, giving off a festive glow that made his younger brother gasp. "Why it's beautiful!" Herman exclaimed in awe.

"Gentlemen," George announced solemnly, "we are witnessing the true dawn of the Age of Electricity."

12

"Let There Be Light"

FOR THE NEXT FIFTEEN DAYS THE LIGHTS IN LAWRENCEVILLE
continued to burn. George stayed on in Massachusetts to
see the results of the endurance test. Each day he and William Stanley visited the building in Lawrenceville to see
how the alternating current system was standing up under
continual use.

They were not disappointed. The thin copper wires did
not burn out as some skeptical Westinghouse engineers had
predicted. The transformers and other apparatus functioned
perfectly without breaking down. Moreover, in spite of the
dangerously high voltage used, there wasn't a single injury
to any of the workmen, because Stanley had insulated the
lines with great care.

At the end of the two-week period, George shut off the
master switch with a decisive gesture and told Stanley, "Well,
Bill, I'm convinced. I think we're ready to demonstrate to
the public what we've come up with."

He wired Herman who had already returned to Pittsburgh
and instructed him to make a public announcement that
Westinghouse alternating current apparatus was available
for commercial use. Then he boarded a train for home,
desperately anxious to see Marguerite and little George
again.

The news that the Westinghouse Electric Company had
found a way to transmit current inexpensively over a long

131

distance rocked the nation. From all over the East, industrial representatives and public officials descended on Great Barrington to observe the alternating current system in operation.

One day George received an urgent message from Stanley that a company had offered to buy the Great Barrington installation, lock, stock and barrel.

"They want it transferred to Buffalo to set up a lighting and power system for the community," Stanley wired. "Shall we sell?"

George wired back, "Sell, by all means. Price isn't important. One commercial installation will do the work of a hundred salesmen."

On Thanksgiving Eve, 1886, Buffalo, New York, became the first city in the world to receive electric light and power on a commercial scale under the Westinghouse system.

George was right. With Buffalo as a showplace for alternating current, orders began to pour in from all sections of the country. Installations were soon completed in dozens of towns and cities, and one industrial town, Greensburg, Pennsylvania, set up a complete municipal plant to provide electrification for all its citizens. The Age of Electricity had begun.

In the two years from 1886 to 1888 the demand for alternating current equipment grew so sharply that the work crew of the Westinghouse Electric Company was forced to expand from two hundred employees to more than three thousand! George observed this amazing growth with gratification—but it was a satisfaction not unmixed with concern. All his life he had equated industrial growth with human progress, with the betterment of living conditions for people everywhere, and he had viewed it in simple terms—as an ageless conflict between growth and stagnation. Never once had he entertained a wisp of a doubt as to the desirability of the triumph of the former over the latter. Now, at the age of forty-two he became aware for perhaps the first time of a new and shadowy dimension to the issue—the evils of social upheaval created by too-rapid industrial development.

He had seen the problem first of all in Pittsburgh itself, which had grown in a few short decades from a small provincial city into a booming industrial center of smoky factories and soot-laden streets. He had seen fine neighborhoods in the very heart of the city deteriorate into industrial slums, and the people who lived in them deteriorate as well. In the crowded, filth-strewn warrens surrounding the factories, crime and disease and alcoholism were exceeded only by the hopelessness of the people. Many were immigrants—Irish, Germans, Poles, Italians—who had come to seek opportunity in the New World, and others were native Americans, newly arrived from the farms or other cities in search of a decent living. They worked long hours in the factories, returning at night to crowded, ramshackle homes devoid of the barest comforts, and they watched in despair as their children grew up spindly-legged and sickly playing on slag heaps and in garbage dumps. Attendance at school was a rarity, and illiteracy was as widespread as disease and delinquency.

Growing increasingly aware of these evils, George asked himself why no one seemed to do anything about the plight of these people. Blame was easy enough to pinpoint—factory owners who located their factories without regard to the effect on surrounding neighborhoods; officeholders interested in catering only to the affluent and politically influential; the apathetic average citizen who did not seem to care what happened to the city so long as it did not affect him personally. George decided that while there was enough fault to go around, the important issue was doing something about it. More specifically, what could *he* as an individual do about it?

He had read that in some of the countries of Europe, notably Denmark and Sweden, interesting experiments were being carried out in the creation of model communities. Slums were being cleared and replaced by decent houses, good schools and sufficient health and hospital facilities. In those countries, forward-looking architects and government officials were no longer content to allow communities to develop haphazardly, in piecemeal fashion, but saw that by carefully laying out in advance all the facilities needed for satisfactory living, families could enjoy a richer, fuller life. Why couldn't this idea be adopted in the United States?

It was a bold idea, but George Westinghouse had long ago learned not to be frightened off by ideas, no matter how farfetched. Why, for example, couldn't an industrialist planning a new factory think not in terms of the factory alone but of an entire factory community? Here was a dream to hang his hat on, he thought with a smile. A model community, complete with modern factory buildings, neat, inexpensive houses for the employees, up-to-date water supply, even a complete electrical power system. In his mind's eye he saw a new industrial town, but one unlike any he had ever seen before. A town with adequate schools, a community center where children and adults could enjoy their leisure time with profit, and a hospital with the finest medical facilities. It would be a town planned from the ground up, dedicated to the proposition that even the lowest-paid factory worker was entitled to share in the fruits of industrial progress.

Soon after, George called in a leading architectural firm and told them that he wanted to move the Westinghouse Air Brake works to a new plant. "I want you to design a factory," he said, "and surround it with a town."

On the advice of the architects a site was selected fourteen miles from Pittsburgh, in an area of low-lying hills where only a few scattered houses dotted the open countryside. In a matter of months the skeleton outline of a new community began to appear, and within two years the model town of Wilmerding, Pennsylvania, was born.

Early in 1890, the air brake works were moved, lock, stock and barrel, from Pittsburgh and installed at Wilmerding. True to George's dream, the community was designed with the welfare of the employees as the paramount consideration. The workshops had the most modern lighting, heating, ventilation and safety facilities. Company houses, neatly land-scaped with grass, trees and shrubbery, were rented to the workers, but carried an option to buy if they chose to do so. Each house was equipped with an indoor bathroom, running water, electric lighting and natural gas outlets for cooking and heating. The schools contained up-to-date educational facilities and were decorated in bright colors to make them attractive to the youngsters, and for recreational purposes a fine community center was available with gymnasiums, library and meeting rooms.

In addition, George instituted a far-reaching plan of workmen's compensation and complete medical and hospital facilities. If an employee fell sick or was injured as the result of an accident, he and his family would be provided for out of the compensation fund, and the finest medical care would be available.

The miracle of Wilmerding and the advanced program of employee benefits soon attracted national attention. Earlier, George had won a reputation as the best boss in Pittsburgh and had earned the resentment of other employers in the area, but with the birth of the model community his reputation spread throughout the country. Dozens of newspapers and magazines sent reporters to write articles about the Westinghouse program.

This was an era of revolutionary changes in labor relations in the United States. Working men and women were just beginning to gain an awareness of their right to demand fair wages and better working conditions from employers, and the latter bitterly fought the attempts of newly formed labor unions to encroach on their ancient prerogatives. It was little wonder, then, that when stories about Wilmerding and George's employee benefits program reached their eyes employers all over the country felt angered and betrayed. They called him a traitor because he had freely and voluntarily given his workers more than even the most militant labor union would ever dream of demanding.

George himself tried his best to ignore the backbiting and

personal attacks. Convinced that his concept of labor relations was just, he declared that he would stick by his guns
and called on other employers to follow a similar policy.
"I believe in competition," he said. "It is the essence of a
free economy. I think employers should compete in improving the lot of their workers as well as in the making of more
and better goods at a cheaper price. It strikes me as common
sense that when men are happy and comfortable they produce more and help make a better profit for the company."

Another of George's radical innovations was a policy of
giving employees in all the Westinghouse companies a half
day off with pay on Saturday. Even his most loyal fellow
directors were dubious about its introduction, for they felt
the expense would be too great. But George told them with
a smile, "When I was a lad in my father's place I vowed that
if I ever had a shop of my own I would give the men Saturday afternoon off at full wages. Call it sentiment if you will,
but I would like you to support me in this boyish whimsy."

The directors voted in favor of the half holiday.

Curiously enough, in spite of his advanced notions about
labor relations—or perhaps because of them—George despised
the concept of charity. He believed firmly in the dignity of
the individual, regardless of income or social position. He
was convinced that charity was damaging to the giver and
the receiver and should be resorted to only when there was
no alternative. "The person who takes the charity thinks
of himself as inferior," he explained. "The donor feels superior. I would rather give a man a chance to *earn* a dollar
than give him five and make him feel he's a 'charity case.'"

Once during a temporary fall-off in business the superintendent of one of the Westinghouse companies announced
it would be necessary to furlough a group of workers.

"How will these men support their families while they're
not working?" George demanded.

The superintendent shrugged and replied, "I don't know."

"In that case keep them on the payroll and give them
something to do."

"Well, we'll keep them on the payroll if you say so, Mr. Westinghouse," the superintendent agreed reluctantly. "But I have no work for them."

"Then create it," George snapped. "Even if it means having them move parts from one end of the shop to another. These men are our employees. They have to eat. But I want them to retain their self-respect, too."

Late in 1890, less than ten months after the creation of Wilmerding, George received sorrowful news. His father had died quietly in his sleep. Grief-stricken, he and Herman rushed to Schenectady to attend the funeral. George prevailed on his mother, who was now nearing eighty, to come and live with him and Marguerite at Solitude. "When we were first married you shared your home with us," he told her. "Now that you're alone I want you to share ours."

Emmeline Westinghouse, white-haired and ailing but still alert, asked cautiously, "And Marguerite? How does she feel about it?"

"It was Marguerite who suggested you come and live with us, Mother," he said simply. So she went to live at Solitude.

The phenomenal growth of the Westinghouse Electric Company created new challenges. The popularity of alternating current was pointing up a need for better equipment, and George was well aware of the problem. "Converting alternating current for use in a direct current motor is satisfactory," he told his associates, "but it's not the final answer. It's inefficient. Find me a good alternating current motor and the inventor can name his own price."

It was Herman who first called his attention to the work of a young engineer, Nikola Tesla, from Serbia. He showed George a clipping from a New York newspaper. It told of a lecture Tesla had delivered before the American Institute of Electric Engineers about his invention of an induction motor which he called a "polyphase alternating current system." The account did not contain too many details, but George decided he wanted to know more about this new motor.

He wrote to Tesla, and in a week he received a reply written in a neat, precise hand. It was a complete description of the alternating current motor, with diagrams. George read the letter carefully. Since he was not a physicist some of the advanced electrical theory was difficult to understand, and he was forced to study the letter a number of times and examine the sketches with great care.

Suddenly, the explanation became clear as a bell. It was as if a haze had disappeared and the concept Tesla was trying to get across was outlined sharply before him. He was hard put to keep from pounding his desk with glee. It was beautiful, this theory of Tesla's, beautiful and simple, once you got the hang of it. What the Serbian-born scientist had done was to eliminate the commutator, brushes and all electrical connections from the armature of the motor, so that the armature could spin freely. It was magnetic lines of force that did the trick. Alternating current going into the motor produced a rotating magnetic field in the field magnet and therefore induced a rotating magnetic field in the armature, too. The "induced field" cause the armature to spin. That was all there was to the motor!

Tesla utilized another trick, too. He introduced in his motor the "polyphase" principle of feeding in two or more alternating current circuits simultaneously, each with a different "phase." It meant that while the circuits were on the same frequency they were out of step with each other, so that there were no dead spots in the operation of the motor and the armature would turn with a steady, uniform motion.

Unless he missed his guess, this man Tesla was an electrical genius, George told himself—a genius he wanted to meet.

Not one to tolerate delay, George acted quickly. He made an appointment to see Tesla and took a train to New York City. He found the inventor in a makeshift laboratory in a small building on Fifth Avenue. On the door was a sign reading "Tesla Electric Company."

Nikola Tesla turned out to be a slim, dark-haired young

man of about thirty, almost as tall as George himself but not nearly so broad and big-boned. He spoke with an accent, but in clipped precise sentences.

From the moment the youthful engineer started to explain his inventions—there were forty patents altogether—it was clear that George's initial estimate of him was correct. Tesla *was* an engineering genius. Unlike George whose own tremendous talents lay in adopting scientific principles for practical use, Tesla's intellectual gifts were in the realm of theory. The man's knowledge of electrical principles was amazing. True, many of his inventions needed additional development before they would be ready for commercial use, but the theories on which they were based were sound and ingenious.

Before he got down to the real purpose of his visit George wanted to know a good deal more about Tesla's background. He learned from the inventor that he had come from the Serbian province of Croatia where his father had been a clergyman. After studying engineering at the Polytechnic Institute at Gratz, Austria, he had gotten a job with the Continental Edison Company in Paris, a French affiliate of the American Edison companies.

A short time later Tesla came to the United States to work for Edison himself in New York City. George wanted to know why he had left his famous employer.

"I do not like to be exploited," was Tesla's frank reply. "Mr. Edison took my inventions and registered them at the patent office in the name of the Edison Company. I received nothing."

George was not entirely surprised for he knew this was a common practice at many companies. Indeed, it was well known that Thomas Edison did not like the men working for him to patent inventions in their own names. Recalling his own unhappy experience with the car replacer and reversible railroad frog George could well understand how young Tesla must have felt.

"So you quit Edison because of that?" he asked.

"That and the fact that Mr. Edison and I had a basic disagreement."

"About what?"

"Electricity," Tesla said. "Mr. Edison thinks only in terms of direct current. I am convinced the real future of electricity lies in alternating current."

"And you argued about it?" George asked.

"It was not precisely an argument," Tesla explained wryly. "You see, Mr. Edison owned the company, I did not. Actually, he could not understand the theory of alternating current. Direct current he could understand, for it is simple and requires little knowledge of abstract electrical theory. But I'm afraid I could never make it clear to him what alternating current was all about."

George smiled. He was beginning to like this self-confident, outspoken young man. "What do you intend to do now?" he inquired.

Tesla indicated the crudely equipped laboratory with a sweeping gesture. "As you can see, I have decided to go into competition with Mr. Edison," he said with the trace of a grin. "Several persons who believe in my inventions have given me financial backing. However, I am afraid I'm an inventor, not a businessman. Things are not going as well as I had hoped. It takes a great deal of money and experience to make a success of business."

The young inventor paused and added, "But tell me, Mr. Westinghouse, you did not come all the way from Pittsburgh to listen to the story of my life. You are far too busy for that."

"Perhaps in a way I did come to learn about you," George observed thoughtfully. "When I do business with someone I want to know about him. You can't separate a man and his ideas."

"You want to do business, sir?" Tesla asked. "With me?"

"Yes, Mr. Tesla," George said. "Like you, I believe in the future of alternating current. I am interested in your induction motor and these other patents you've described since they all have to do with alternating current. There are forty?"

"That is correct, Mr. Westinghouse."

"I want to buy them all."

"All?" Tesla asked in astonishment.

"Yes, *all*," George repeated. "For cash and a royalty. I believe a man should be paid for what he creates with his brain."

"Well, I hadn't quite expected that you would want to—" Tesla began uncertainly, losing his self-assurance for the first time.

"I'm prepared to offer you a million dollars for all your patents," George said quietly. "Plus a royalty of one dollar per horsepower used. I think that's very fair."

For a moment he thought the young inventor was about to faint. Tesla's face turned white and he held on to a workbench to steady himself. Finally he found his voice and said, "You'll have to excuse me, Mr. Westinghouse, but I am not used to hearing such sums of money offered to me. Indeed, I have never been remotely connected with business discussions of this magnitude."

"If you think it's too much money—that I'm cheating myself—don't be deluded," George replied bluntly. "I'm buying your patents because I need them and can exploit them to good advantage. I assure you that for the Westinghouse Electric Company it will prove to be a profitable investment. Now what do you say, Mr. Tesla, will you accept my offer?"

Nikola Tesla nodded without saying another word.

13

Battle of the Giants

DURING THE YEARS THAT GEORGE WESTINGHOUSE WORKED ON his alternating current system, Thomas Alva Edison was proceeding along other lines. Convinced that direct current was superior, he concerned himself with its development exclusively, refusing even to entertain the notion that alternating current might be more practical. Whether it was from an inability to understand the theory behind alternating current, as Nikola Tesla had maintained, or whether it was due to pigheadedness, as some of his other critics liked to believe, Edison continued to pour his resources into direct current. And for a time he managed to dominate electrical development in a few of the large cities through the formation of a giant corporation known as the Edison General Electric Company.

The growth of two divergent electrical systems held out the prospect of a clash in the future. George knew this only too well, but in spite of the threat of a nasty controversy he was willing to gamble completely on his own faith in alternating current.

This, then, was the picture in the field of electrical development when George returned to Pittsburgh early in 1891 after purchasing the rights to the Tesla patents. He assigned his engineers to make a careful study of the alternating current motor, and the reports of the exhaustive tests bore out his own preliminary conclusion that changes would have to be made before it could be put into commercial production.

The most difficult task lay in adapting the motor to the 133-cycle frequency which George had established as standard for the alternating current system. Tesla had designed his models to operate on a lower 60-cycle frequency, believing this would produce maximum efficiency for polyphase operation. But the Westinghouse engineers argued that it was less expensive to redesign the motor to operate on 133 cycles than to change the standard frequency.

George decided to go along with his engineers. "We'll ask Tesla to change the design," he told them. "Since the motor is his invention, he deserves first crack at it."

Tesla was summoned to Pittsburgh and arrived carrying a battered suitcase and an armful of dog-eared books on electrical theory. He went to work at once, but the job proved to be harder than anyone had suspected. "It will take time and money," Tesla reported after the first week.

"Take all the time you need," George replied. "The important thing is to do the job. Remember, someday your motor will be used in every home and factory. It will drive sewing machines and lathes and equipment of every description. Even streetcars and underground railways will run on electricity, because of the Tesla motor."

In spite of George's faith, things did not go well. Tesla, the temperamental wizard who had worked alone in the past, had sharp disagreements with the other engineers that grew into bitter quarrels. George tried to soothe ruffled feelings on both sides but was unsuccessful. Even when he was able to negotiate a truce it proved to be temporary and soon the arguments would start again. Eventually, work on the motor came to a standstill.

Just about this time George suddenly found himself in the midst of other difficulties. The long-threatened clash with the Edison interests broke out into the open like a bursting storm cloud.

Earlier, Tom Edison and his direct-current supporters had

laughed off the alternating current threat. They were not even disturbed when they learned that the Westinghouse company was making inroads into the smaller towns and rural areas, for the expense of generating and distributing direct current was so high that the less populous districts did not constitute a profitable market for General Electric.

As the Westinghouse organization expanded and began to invade the New York market, the earlier amusement of the Edison group changed to concern. New York was the direct current capital. If an upstart company like Westinghouse could challenge the mighty Edison corporation on its own doorstep, perhaps alternating current was a serious threat after all.

The direct current interests began a full-scale publicity and advertising campaign to undermine public confidence in alternating current. The earlier natural gas controversy proved to be a minor skirmish compared to the bitter warfare waged on the issue of electricity.

General Electric spent thousands of dollars to fill newspapers, magazines and billboards with advertisements condemning alternating current as a public menace. They charged that since it was transmitted at high voltages, men, women and children were threatened with injury and death. George tried to counter the damaging onslaught by explaining that transformers stepped down the voltage after transmission, thus making it perfectly safe for use in the home. But the Edison interests continued their attack. A newspaper story about a lad who had been killed after accidentally touching a low-hanging high-tension wire was exploited to the hilt. General Electric warned parents that alternating current constituted a threat to the life of *every* American child. Some of the newspapers sympathetic to the Edison point of view, or heavily dependent on advertising revenue from General Electric, played up the story with the most lurid headlines they could devise.

As the controversy grew more heated, Thomas Edison personally entered the fray by writing an article for the well-known magazine *North American Review* entitled "The Dangers of Electric Lighting." In it he strongly condemned alternating current, declaring that no known method of insulation could render a high-tension wire safe. In the following month's issue George published "A Reply to Mr. Edison."

"The alternating current will kill people, of course," he explained. "So will gunpowder, and dynamite, and whisky and a lot of other things; but we have a system whereby the deadly electricity of alternating current can do no harm unless a man is fool enough to swallow a whole dynamo."

Before long the argument grew so bitter that charges of bribery, fraud and criminal libel were hurled back and forth by some of the less restrained supporters on both sides.

Yet in spite of the powerful forces arrayed against it, the alternating current concept gained momentum. Sales of Westinghouse equipment boomed and orders for electrical installations continued to pour in from all sections of the country.

At the crucial moment when the battle was beginning to go in George's favor something happened that threatened to write a disastrous finish to the alternating current story. The prison officials of New York State announced that electrocution would replace hanging as the method of executing prisoners condemned to death!

In their effort to find the surest, quickest and most painless form of execution, medical experts appointed by New York officials had proposed an "electric chair" powered by alternating current stepped up to high voltages.

It was a perfect weapon for the enemies of alternating current, made possible by the development of the Westinghouse transformer. For George this was a grim bit of irony.

The Edison interests gleefully renewed the attack. What better proof was there that alternating current was a menace than its selection by New York State as the official mode of execution? they asked. The theme was repeated again and again. In newspapers, magazines and lectures they tried to link death and alternating current in the public mind.

At the height of the propaganda battle George received a troubling report from his brother Herman. The cost of redesigning the Tesla motor was draining off a good deal of the Westinghouse Electric Company's reserve funds.

"Is that all?" George asked wearily.

"It's serious enough," Herman said. "The company's financial picture is not good. Our rapid growth plus the cost of the Tesla motor project has drained us dry. We need cash desperately."

George studied the financial statement Herman had handed him and said, "But sales are holding up, and our profit picture is strong."

"That's true," Herman admitted, "but we must have reserves badly, particularly if we have to weather a dry spell as a result of this latest electric-chair scare."

George nodded. "I think you're right. We'll have to float a loan. That shouldn't be difficult, considering the strength of our assets."

George called a meeting of some of the leading bankers in the Pittsburgh area. After explaining his predicament, he asked them to advance the needed funds. The bankers pointed out that because of the size of the loan no one bank could handle it alone—it would have to be done on a syndicate basis. George told them he had no objection if they wished to pool their resources.

As they were about to negotiate the details of the loan, one of the bankers said, "Of course, Mr. Westinghouse, we will want the power to name a general manager for your company."

George was taken aback. "I don't understand," he replied. "The management of the company is my affair."

"Not quite, sir. If we are to risk our funds we want assurances—"

"But the assets of the company are your collateral," George protested. "You've seen reports of our financial structure and outlook for the future. The company is a healthy, expanding organization. What further assurances do you need?"

"I'm afraid it's not that simple, Mr. Westinghouse," the spokesman for the bankers said. "We've studied your management policies and frankly we're not satisfied. A more businesslike approach is indicated. I think I speak for all of us, do I not, gentlemen?" He turned to his colleagues for support. They nodded in unanimous agreement.

"Specifically, what do you object to?" George asked, trying to retain a calm exterior.

"For one thing, your preoccupation with research. One of the reasons you're short of cash is your heavy investment in the development of new equipment, such as this polyphase motor device. If you limited your activities to manufacturing and selling equipment that has been proven commercially sound, the company would be on far more solid ground, financially."

Westinghouse set his jaw and declared slowly, "Without research there would be no transformer, no alternating current equipment—indeed, there would be no Westinghouse Electric Company. Progress is our most important commodity. We invent and develop new and better things for the long-range benefit of the nation and its people. I am an inventor. Financial profit alone does not intrigue me. If ever the time comes when that is the only concern of the Westinghouse Electric Company I will no longer be associated with it. Is that clear, gentlemen?"

"But we're businessmen, Mr. Westinghouse," the banker argued. "We have to protect ourselves. You must understand our position."

"I understand it perfectly well," George said firmly. "Since I am not a banker, I would never presume to tell you how to run your bank. Similarly, I will not permit anyone to tell me how to run my company."

"Under those circumstances you realize that we cannot grant your request for a loan," the banker declared.

"I am aware of that," Westinghouse replied. "Thank you for giving me your time. Good day, gentlemen."

With no chance of securing the necessary funds in Pittsburgh, the company was threatened with a crisis. George called in Herman and the other officers for a strategy discussion. At that meeting he disclosed an alternate plan.

"I intend to go to New York City and discuss the matter with some of the bankers there," he informed them. "Perhaps they'll lend us the money without trying to dominate us."

Some of his colleagues were dubious. "Why New York is the very heart of Edison territory," one of the directors observed. "The bankers will turn us down flat."

"I don't think so," George argued. "It's precisely because they are in New York that I want to approach them. I've been studying the situation there. It's an interesting one. Apparently Edison and his backers are so big they've been able to dictate to the banking institutions on their own terms. Some of the independent banks are resentful. They might be willing to help us, if only to encourage competition in order to keep General Electric from becoming too powerful."

"I agree with George," Herman said. "It's worth a try." The directors voted to go ahead with the plan.

Before he could make arrangements to go to New York, George received a surprising letter. It was from C. A. Coffin, president of the Edison General Electric Company, and requested a meeting on a "vital matter."

He showed the letter to Herman, who was wary. "Coffin's reputation is well known," he told George. "He must be planning some piece of nasty business. Let's be on our guard."

George tapped his desk thoughtfully and declared, "Yes, but we owe it to ourselves to find out what is on his mind."

He sent a formal reply to the General Electric head in New York agreeing to a meeting in Pittsburgh.

Coffin showed up a few days later. In physique and personality he was the direct opposite of Westinghouse. While George was tall and heavily built, Coffin was small and slight. He spoke quickly and in a high-pitched voice. Throughout their conversation his eyes, hidden behind a pair of rimless spectacles, darted shrewdly about, taking in every detail of George's office.

The General Electric head did not come directly to the point but proceeded to give a detailed history of his company's development. He boasted how he had gradually absorbed most of the independent companies into one giant corporation. Then he confided smugly how he had squeezed out the two inventors, Thomson and Houston, whose patents formed the basis for General Electric's success.

George guessed Coffin was revealing all this to frighten him into believing that General Electric was too big and powerful for an independent company like Westinghouse to oppose. Coffin's next words confirmed his suspicion.

"So you see, Mr. Westinghouse, we're not exactly amateurs," the New Yorker went on. "We've fought a great many battles and my company has always come out on top. I happen to know the present dispute between our two organizations has hurt you considerably."

"What do you mean?" George inquired guardedly.

"I know, for example, that your company's liquid reserves are low and you've had to apply for loans," Coffin replied with a thin smile, as if he had just played a trump card.

"How do you know this?"

"As I said before, we are not amateurs at this sort of game. We have our sources of information."

"What do you have in mind?" George asked.

"Ah, now we get down to brass tacks," Coffin said. "I have a proposition to put to you. If this fight continues both of our companies will lose money. What I have in mind is an arrangement—"

"What sort of arrangement?" George demanded suspiciously.

"A confidential arrangement," Coffin declared without blinking an eye. "An agreement—not on paper, mind you— whereby rates and prices for electricity would be set and adhered to by both of us. The market for power and equip-

ment would be divided on a sort of territorial basis. In that
way our activities would not intrude on each other, prices
would be fixed to yield a handsome profit and other companies would be shut out of the market."

George was incensed at the bald arrogance of the man.
"What you are proposing is a secret monopoly to fix prices
and business practices," he asserted flatly. "Am I right?"

"That's a harsh way of putting it, Mr. Westinghouse,"
Coffin protested uncomfortably.

"But it's the truth, isn't it," George retorted angrily. "You
want to do away with the traditional American principle of
open competition. Well, I happen to believe competition in
business is a sound principle. Without it there would be no
industrial progress or growth. I've adhered to that concept
all my life, and I don't intend to betray it now. It's only
through competition that prices are kept low and the public
benefits. I shall continue to fight with all my strength against
this wretched moral sickness that has infected so many of
our business leaders. 'The public be damned,' they say. Well
I say that is the ethic of the pickpocket and highwayman,
regardless of the finery worn by the individual who utters it."

Coffin paled but said nothing.

"Moreover," George added contemptuously, "you tell me
how you cheated Thomson and Houston out of their patent
rights! Why should I trust you after what you tell me?"

The General Electric president rose, put on his handsome
coat and said in a strained voice, "Good day, Mr. Westinghouse."

"Good day," George replied grimly. He could feel his
facial muscles twitching in anger.

Later he gave Herman a detailed account of the meeting.
"Do you think it was wise to lose your temper?" his brother
asked. "After all, Coffin is a powerful man. Now he'll be
doubly angry and twice as dangerous."

"Perhaps I did speak out impulsively," George admitted
with a wry smile. "It's been a long time since I've blown up
like that, but I was truly angry. You know, Herman, steam

engines have to have safety valves or explode. We humans should learn to let off steam, too. Sometimes it's good for the soul."

The following day George was on his way to New York City to float the needed loan. Three days later the Westinghouse directors received a telegraph message from him informing them that he had met with a group of independent New York bankers and had succeeded in getting them to advance funds to the Westinghouse Electric Company with no strings attached!

14

A Glimpse of Tomorrow

SHORTLY AFTER HIS RETURN FROM NEW YORK CITY WESTING-house called in Tesla. "Nikola, I want your frank estimate of our chances of redesigning your motor for the standard hundred-and-thirty-three-cycle frequency," he said bluntly. "If you feel the problem can be licked I'm willing to continue with the project, even if it means more time and money. But I must know what our chances are."

"You ask for my honest opinion, so I'll give it to you," the inventor told him. "I think you're better off if you abandon the project and reconvert the standard current to suit the motor, rather than the other way around."

Westinghouse frowned and said, "You feel it's hopeless, then?"

"I did not say that," Tesla replied in his precise way. "Oh, in time the problem might be worked out, but the chances are remote."

"Why didn't you tell me this at the beginning, when I first called you to Pittsburgh?"

"Because I am a scientist, Mr. Westinghouse," the younger man said. "I was reasonably certain the sixty-cycle frequency I used was the most efficient, but I couldn't be certain, not without additional experimentation. Well, we have conducted the experiments, dozens of experiments, as you know. We have had bitter arguments about them, your engineers and I. Now I am convinced the only practical solution is to continue with my original sixty-cycle operation."

Westinghouse furrowed his brow in deep thought. It was not an easy decision to make, abandoning the redevelopment project after investing so much time and effort. Particularly since the cost had been an important factor in the company's present financial troubles. It would mean having to admit to the stockholders that he had failed. Yet wasn't all scientific advancement nothing more than an endless process of weeding out past errors? If man was to succeed in bettering his lot he must first learn how to admit to mistakes, George mused.

He said quietly, "I think you're right, Nikola. We will abandon the project and get to work at once on reconverting to a new standard frequency of sixty cycles for general use."

Tesla didn't blink an eye. "I thought you would say that, Mr. Westinghouse," he said simply. "Do not think I'm unaware of the magnitude of your decision. It's not easy for a man in your position to have to admit an expensive undertaking has failed. But like me you are an inventor, and inventors cannot afford the luxury of false pride or self-delusion."

Even with the adoption of the sixty-cycle system Westinghouse knew there would have to be a few modifications in the polyphase motor before it could go into commercial production. So he asked how soon it could be readied for manufacture. At this point Tesla dropped a bombshell by announcing that he was leaving Pittsburgh.

"But why, Nikola?" Westinghouse asked.

"Because the minor changes are simple enough," Tesla replied. "Your engineers can make them as well as I. There is no further purpose in my remaining here."

Then he added wryly, "Besides, your engineers and I are not exactly on the friendliest of terms. If I were to stay, there would be additional disputes about minor issues, and that would hamper instead of help."

Tesla left Pittsburgh, but only after promising to return

if the company ran into an unexpected problem that required his expert knowledge. Marguerite and George saw him off at the railroad station. Just before the train pulled out Nikola declared, "Remember—if you need me, telegraph and I shall be here in a matter of hours."

Westinghouse turned his attention once more to the problem of meeting the challenge of the direct current advocates. The Edison General Electric Company had exploited the electrocution issue with devastating effectiveness. So well organized was the anti-Westinghouse propaganda that it began to look as if public opinion, which for a time had begun to favor alternating current, was now reversing itself.

George thought long and hard about the problem. What was needed, he decided, was an opportunity to demonstrate publicly the innate superiority of alternating current. He recalled his earlier success in winning support for his air brake by outfitting a special train and taking it on a tour of various cities. Unfortunately, electricity did not lend itself to this sort of traveling demonstration. But what if he found some other way of dramatizing the superiority of alternating current? It would have to be an effort on a grand scale, a demonstration that would capture the attention of the entire civilized world and kindle the imagination of people everywhere.

One morning George arrived at his office early to find a youthful member of his engineering staff, Lewis B. Stillwell, waiting to see him. Stillwell had just returned from a technical meeting in London, and explained that while in England he met an American named E. D. Adams who was head of the Cataract Construction Company, one of the leading contracting firms in the United States.

"Adams wants to sponsor a competition," Stillwell said.

"What sort of competition?"

"A contest to select a plan to harness Niagara Falls!" the youthful engineer exuberated. "Adams thinks the water power can be made to generate enough electricity to supply light and power for all of northern New York State."

Westinghouse whistled and replied, "That's a big order."

"I thought you'd be interested, sir," Stillwell went on eagerly. "Shall I write to Adams to tell him the Westinghouse Electric Company will submit a plan?"

"Not so fast, Stillwell," George cautioned. "There are several aspects that must be explored before we commit ourselves. For example, what fee does this man Adams offer?"

"Why, none, Mr. Westinghouse. It's a competition. The winning company receives a three-thousand-dollar prize."

"And no guarantee that it will also be awarded the contract, even if it submits the best plan?"

Stillwell paused, then admitted reluctantly, "I suppose that's right, sir. Frankly, I was so excited by the idea I never stopped to worry about details."

"Well, Stillwell, you've learned something from this—that in our business details are important," George said wryly. "These people are trying to secure a hundred thousand dollars' worth of information for three thousand dollars. That's wrong in principle, and in all conscience I couldn't agree to such an arrangement. However, if and when they are ever ready to negotiate on a more businesslike basis we'll submit our plans."

As Stillwell left the office, somewhat crestfallen, George stared pensively up at the ceiling. Harnessing Niagara Falls for electricity! The most famous waterfalls in the world. It was a tremendously exciting prospect. And what an opportunity to prove the potentials of alternating current! Indeed, it was just the chance he had been searching for, and yet to submit plans under the terms set forth by Adams was impossible. No, George told himself, he would bide his time patiently like a good fisherman and perhaps find a better way to hook the fish. . . .

One evening at dinner Marguerite asked George if he had seen the afternoon newspapers.

"No, dear," he replied, reaching for a slice of bread. "I've been too busy. Was there something I should have seen?"

"Nothing earth-shaking," she said, "but it was announced

that the next World's Fair will be held in Chicago, in 1893. It's going to be called the Columbian Exposition in honor of the four-hundredth anniversary of the discovery of America. It promises to be a wonderful fair. Just think, that's only two years from now. Little George will be nine, exactly the right age to enjoy it. Do you remember the marvelous time we had at the Centennial Exposition in Philadelphia?"

"I do, indeed," George said thoughtfully. "That was fifteen years ago. How quickly the years fly!"

After dinner he picked up the newspaper and turned to the story about the Fair. Marguerite was right. It promised to be a thrilling event, and young George would have the time of his life at the Exposition.

Midway in the article George paused to reread a paragraph. It stated that tentative plans called for the World's Fair to be illuminated by electricity. "This would be an unprecedented step," the story said. "So far, no information concerning the details of the electrifying process has been received by this newspaper."

George leaned back in his easy chair and let his imagination soar. In his mind's eye he saw a magic city of light. It was a dazzling array of splendid buildings, magnificent gardens and exhibit halls dedicated to the growth of America. It was a city illumined by hundreds of thousands of lamps, all powered by electricity—the most gigantic lighting project of its kind ever undertaken. In truth, here was a challenge to test the efficiency of alternating current as it had never been tested before—an ideal opportunity to capture the attention and imagination of the entire civilized world.

The next morning George called a meeting of the directors. With dramatic word images he painted for them a picture of the vision he'd had. He told them of a city of light surrounded by a man-made aurora while thousands of lamps flicked on and off like bright stars glittering in the soft darkness of a summer's night.

When he finished there was a long silence. Finally someone said, "It sounds grand, Mr. Westinghouse, so grand that it frightens one to think of undertaking such a project."

Herman observed, "It's the type of project that will tax all our resources, and then we may find we are unable to carry it through. It could mean bankruptcy. Are we prepared to risk that?"

"Yes, the risks are high," George replied thoughtfully. "But the stakes are worth it. I am all for going ahead. Are you with me, gentlemen?"

Silently, the directors began to lift their hands in affirmation. One, two, three, four . . . When Herman, who was tallying the vote, finished his count every hand in the room was raised. The proposal had been endorsed unanimously.

George got to work immediately. He dispatched a team of engineers to Chicago to survey the site and obtain the lighting specifications from the directors of the Fair. They returned ten days later with some interesting news. The exposition would require two hundred and fifty thousand lamps. More than a half dozen companies had already submitted bids, including the giant Edison General Electric combine. Finally, the task would require special apparatus and equipment that had not yet been designed. Did Mr. Westinghouse still intend to go ahead in the face of these obstacles? the senior engineer asked.

"Of course," George retorted firmly. "Especially since you tell me Coffin and his General Electric people are also after the prize. This may be the crucial battleground. What figure did General Electric quote for the contract?"

"They asked for a minimum of thirteen dollars and ninety-eight cents per light for each of the two hundred and fifty thousand lamps," the engineer replied.

"Very well," George nodded. "I want you to get to work at once on the preliminary plans and estimates so we can submit a bid within a week, even if it means working your men night and day."

When the estimates were completed Westinghouse went before his board of directors again and explained the specifications. He announced that the cost to the Westinghouse

Electric Company would be only $5.25 per lamp, as compared
to the General Electric bid of $13.98!

The directors were jubilant. "This finally and definitely
proves that alternating current is more efficient than direct
current," one director declared happily. "Even if we add
on a healthy profit we'll outdo Coffin's bid by an impressive
figure. Tell me, George, what do you feel is an adequate
margin of profit?"

"In this case, none," George replied. "I intend to submit
our cost as the bid price."

"What?" the director protested incredulously. "You're
going to offer to take the project at five twenty-five per lamp?
Why that not only leaves us no profit, it doesn't even provide
a margin of reserve, in case our estimate is low, or if we are
suddenly beset by an emergency. We may wind up losing
money! That's not sound business, not by a long shot."

"Not only is it sound, but it will prove to be the best
investment the Westinghouse Electric Company ever made,"
George said calmly. "Listen to me, gentlemen. Our one goal
at the moment is to prove as effectively as we know how
that alternating current is superior to direct current for general use. The lower our bid the more dramatic the effect.
Don't you see, even if we lose some money on this project
we have the opportunity to demonstrate to the entire world
that our principles of electrification are superior."

Once again the board of directors gave George a vote of
confidence. Two weeks later the World's Fair committee announced that the Westinghouse bid had won.

The following months were a time of hectic activity. Almost the entire resources of the company were marshaled to
meet the monumental task of providing electrification for
the Fair. At first the Edison interests had been stunned and
bewildered by the fantastically low figure quoted by Westinghouse. Now they set out to keep George from completing
his end of the agreement.

One of Coffin's key moves was to initiate a court action
prohibiting the Westinghouse company from manufacturing

"all-glass-globe" lamps. George had earlier purchased rights to an incandescent bulb known as the Sawyer-Man lamp, since he knew his rivals would never license him to manufacture Edison lamps or sell him a supply. Through a shrewd legal gambit the General Electric lawyers sought an injunction against the manufacture of the Sawyer-Man lamp on the grounds that it infringed on the Edison patents. George felt sure he could win the court fight, but he also knew it would take time—perhaps years—before the suit was settled, and time was a commodity he could not afford.

With customary zeal he set to work with his engineers devising a two-piece lamp which could not under any circumstances be considered an infringement on existing patents. Within a month they came up with a "stopper lamp" consisting of two pieces of glass and a soft iron filament which actually cost less than the standard Edison lamp! Next, George organized a company to produce two hundred and fifty thousand lamps and large quantities of replacements; and finally he designed an air pump to exhaust the bulbs, as well as apparatus to fit the pieces together.

To provide electricity for the Fair the Westinghouse engineers installed twelve huge generators, each of which produced a thousand horsepower of alternating current. In addition to the lighting George also ordered an elaborate exhibit of Westinghouse products to be set up on the Fair grounds. It included a complete Tesla polyphase system including induction motors, transformers and model generators. It showed on a miniature scale how alternating current could be transmitted great distances to serve the needs of the public. Through simple diagrams and placards it explained the precautions taken to eliminate the danger from high-voltage transmission.

On the balmy morning of May 1, 1893, George, Marguerite and little George stood at the entrance to the Columbian Exposition in Chicago and waited with mounting excitement for Grover Cleveland, President of the United States, to press the key signifying the opening of the great

fair. Finally a cheer rose from the multitude that had gathered at the entrance. "It's open!" people shouted. "The Fair
is open!"

As they were swept into the grounds the Westinghouse
family gazed on a glamorous city of giant buildings, land-
scaped gardens and exotic lagoons. Nine-year-old George
grasped his father's hand tightly and stared wide-eyed at a
reproduction of a volcano that spouted realistic flame, smoke
and lava. He pointed to a giant wheel carrying people high
in the air and shouted excitedly over the loud, brassy music
of the midway, "What is that, Father?"

George stroked the boy's hair fondly. "A new invention,
made especially to entertain boys and girls—and sometimes
grownups, too," he explained with a sly wink at Marguerite.
"They call it a Ferris Wheel. Why don't we take a ride
in it?"

All morning and afternoon they rode the breathtaking
rides, many newly designed for the Exposition, joined in the
laughter of the huge crowds at the antics of the performers
in the amusement booths and listened in fascination to the
hawking of the gravel-voiced barkers and candy butchers.
Young George consumed so much caramel corn and taffy
that by late afternoon Marguerite called a halt for fear he
would be sick to his stomach.

They visited Machinery Hall where the latest machines
and inventions were on exhibit, and here in microcosm they
viewed the industrial history of the last quarter century. It
was a far more beautiful fair than the Centennial Exposition
of seventy-six. There were the latest McCormick farming
machines, which did everything but actually grow the crops;
giant new printing presses that operated on a rotary principle
and could turn out thousands of newspapers an hour; and
specialized machinery for manufacturing dozens of different
products, from soap to firearms. Also on display at the fair
was a box-shaped camera called a "kodak," designed by a
George Eastman, that could take a photograph at the press
of a button; a machine known as a typewriter that was just

becoming popular for business offices; and several experimental models of clumsy-looking carriages which allegedly
could be driven by a new type of engine powered by a
petroleum derivative, "gasoline."

Exciting as the Exposition was by day it was even more
fascinating at night. The thousands of glowing bulbs illuminated the grounds brilliantly, and the sight evoked astonished
oh's and ah's from the awed crowds. Little George stared
at the magnificent scene and was so carried away that he
called out proudly in a loud voice, "My father made those
lights," and he repeated it until George, flushed with embarrassment, ordered him to hush.

Late that night, when they left the fairgrounds, George
stared down at his young son and somehow the worry and
weariness of the past months of work were forgotten. His
own contribution to the success of the Exposition had been
sizable. The cost had been great in terms of the physical
and mental demands it had made on him. Yet the radiant
expression on his son's face was reward enough.

The Westinghouse family spent two weeks in Chicago,
although Marguerite worried endlessly that young George
would miss too much schoolwork. She wanted them to return
after the first week, but George took a more lenient view
of the matter and sympathized with the youngster when the
boy pleaded that they remain another week.

They had gotten special permission for little George to
miss five days of classes and had taken along his books so
he would not be too far behind on his return. Westinghouse, however, pointed out that it would be a shame for
George to miss seeing the Exposition in its entirety. "It's
far too much to see in a single week," he told his wife. "Besides, this too is an important part of George's education,
and he may not have another chance like this in his lifetime."

Marguerite relented, but only after her husband agreed
to write to the school asking that the leave be extended. As
an added condition, George promised to help the youngster

with his studies, so every evening after returning to their hotel suite he spent an hour or two instructing the boy in his lessons.

When they finally returned to Pittsburgh, George found his desk piled high with reports, memoranda and other papers. But as soon as he was caught up with his work he began to look restlessly about for a new project to tackle.

He didn't have to search far. One morning a letter arrived from E. D. Adams, president of the Cataract Construction Company. The letter explained that one of the engineers for Cataract had just returned from the World's Fair where he had had a chance to examine the Westinghouse alternating current system at close hand.

"I regret that our man missed you," the letter went on. "Apparently he arrived in Chicago just after you had left. In any case we have considered your system and feel that it may offer the most suitable and efficient method for the development of power resources at Niagara Falls. If you and your engineers can devise a plan for the installation of generating equipment we will be happy to discuss a contract."

The patience of the fisherman had paid off, George thought with a smile. The fish had taken the hook. . . .

He immediately assigned young Stillwell to head a team to prepare blueprints, sketches and estimates. Within a few weeks the proposal was sent off to Adams. On October 27, 1893, Westinghouse received a letter from the Cataract Company informing him that his plan for the development of Niagara Falls—the most spectacular project of electrical power development ever attempted—had been accepted.

15

The New Era

GRATIFIED AT HAVING BEEN AWARDED THE NIAGARA PROJECT,
George nevertheless wondered why Adams wrote him instead
of selecting a "winner" through the competition he had
sponsored. Nor could he understand why Edison General
Electric had not shown an interest in the project.

It was not until he met Adams in person that he learned
what had really happened. The head of the Cataract Construction Company confided that while many proposals for
Niagara development had been submitted—some quite bizarre—not one had proved practical. So the contest had been
a failure.

"I'm surprised the Edison people didn't bid for the job,"
George wondered. "From past experience I'd have expected
them to fight for it tooth and nail."

"They did," Adams told him. "And an elaborate plan
it was, too. Sixty pages of specifications, a dozen exhibits,
and I can't recall how many blueprints, sketches and photographs."

"What was wrong with it?"

"It was a direct current system," Adams replied. "I was
impressed—until I received the report on your polyphase
system at the World's Fair. I realized then that Westinghouse alternating current was the electricity of the future."

This was important news. For the second time the Edison
interests had lost out on a major project. No wonder they had

remained discreetly silent. Now, for the first time, George could sniff the heady air of ultimate victory.

The initial order for the Niagara installation called for three mammoth generators, each capable of producing five thousand horsepower of electricity. The first was to be installed within twenty-four months.

"I want to beat that deadline, if possible," George told his engineers. "Use all the men you need, but get the job done as soon as possible."

The first unit was installed in eighteen months. Early in 1895, an impressive gathering that included George, Herman, the heads of the Cataract Company, famous engineers from all over the world and public officials representing the United States and Canada gathered at Niagara Falls to witness a demonstration of the new dynamo installation.

George stared out at the magnificent falls with a curious mingling of awe and humility. Tears of emotion welled up in his eyes. For twenty-five thousand years the roaring waters of the Niagara River had rushed headlong down the precipitous drop of one hundred and sixty feet, breaking pure white against the boulders below and sending up a great veil of misty spray. It was Nature showing off her power in its most primitive form, full of grandeur and beauty, limitless and forbidding. For how many centuries, George wondered, had men stood where he was standing now and dreamed of harnessing those mighty falls to human needs. In that brief moment he had the giddy sensation of standing on the threshold of history.

His reverie was interrupted by Adams' voice announcing that the dynamos were about to be turned on. Quietly George gave a signal to Lewis Stillwell who had directed the project, and the young engineer pulled a master switch. The powerful machines came to life with a smooth steady hum, while in the background like some orchestral accompaniment the falls themselves roared their mighty song.

"I do not intend to speak at length," George told the assembled guests when speeches were in order. "It would be presumptuous and unnecessary. The event today speaks for itself. What we are witnessing here is a development that will ultimately affect the lives of all the peoples in all the countries of the world."

The initial order for three generators was soon increased to ten, and power plants were constructed on both sides of the falls. Power lines, stretching through western and middle New York State and eastern Canada, carried electricity for lighting, heating and industrial purposes into thousands of homes and factories.

George's triumph was marred by the death of his mother after a long illness. She had been in considerable pain the last few months, and George and Marguerite knew that death actually had been merciful. But for little George, who was only eleven, it was the first real tragedy of his life to learn that his beloved grandmother who had lived with them was gone forever.

To help the youngster adjust to what he could not fully comprehend, George took the family to New York City for a week's holiday. Shortly after their arrival he was amazed to receive a call from his old rival Coffin. The head of General Electric asked in a friendly way if they might meet for dinner.

Recalling the last "important business" he had discussed with Coffin, George viewed his call with cynicism, but curiosity got the better of him and he agreed to the meeting.

The General Electric president came right to the point. "I'm going to put all my cards on the table," he said solemnly. "It's now clear to Mister Edison, myself and the rest of our associates that in fighting alternating current we are committed to a losing cause. Frankly, Mister Westinghouse, I've come to ask you to license my company to use the alternating current patents which you control. In return we'll extend to you the right to use our patents. It will be done under a straight exchange and royalty basis."

"Are you proposing another 'secret agreement?'" George countered. "If so, I'm still not interested."

"No," Coffin said with a thin smile. "We know we are beaten. This would be open and aboveboard. A patent control committee would be appointed representing both our companies. The terms of the agreement would be announced publicly, and so would the names of the committee members. Our attorneys would make certain that the agreement is not in violation of the antitrust laws. Is that satisfactory?"

"Yes," George said, "just as long as the interests of the public as well as our respective companies are protected."

"I assure you we are prepared to go all the way in that regard," Coffin insisted.

The following year, 1896, after many months of negotiation, officials of the Westinghouse Electric Company and the Edison General Electric Company affixed their signatures to a document setting up a Patent Control Board. Afterward George told Herman with a grin, "Well, the truce has been signed. The war of the currents is over."

As the world got ready to enter a new century the activities of the Westinghouse company continued to expand. Armed with patents for Westinghouse signaling devices and transformers, the Tesla induction motor and other alternating current equipment, George entered the brand new field of railway electrification. The firm began to manufacture installations for electrically-powered trolley cars, elevated trains and underground "rapid transit" systems for large cities like New York and London.

The increasing demand for electrical power for home, industry and transportation gave rise to a new interest. George envisioned a time when present methods of generating electricity would be outmoded. A staunch advocate of the principle that new advances in science and industry brought with them the need for additional progress, he liked to say, "The more things we invent, the more things we need to invent," wryly referring to it as "Westinghouse's Law."

As demands for power increased, the size of generators grew larger, and so did the steam engines—or "prime movers"

—that turned the dynamos. But the principle of operation remained the same. The prime movers were still the old-fashioned type of reciprocating engine that had been used in his father's shop forty years before. By the late 1890's they had grown so large and unwieldy that George was convinced they had reached the maximum limits of their usefulness.

What was needed, he decided, was a smaller engine of high speed and efficiency to enable power stations to double, triple or quadruple electrical output. "We have twentieth-century motors, lamps and other devices for using electricity," he observed to his board of directors, "but we're twenty years behind the times in supplying power for these devices."

It came to him suddenly that the problem was not unrelated to the one he had tried to solve as a boy, when he had invented his rotary engine! He had wondered then why it was necessary to convert back-and-forth motion from a reciprocating steam engine to rotating motion to spin a simple shaft when a rotary engine would do the job more efficiently. Didn't the same principle hold true for turning a dynamo?

True, there had been so much else to do over the years that he had never gotten around to translating his boyhood dream into a commercial reality. But the rotary concept that had been the basis for his very first patent was still sound. In fact, somewhere in the basement of Solitude was the model ship he and Hanson, the carpenter on board the *Muscoota*, had used to test his little engine thirty-five years before.

One Sunday afternoon he and young George went down to the storage room to search through closets, shelves and half-forgotten trunks. At last they found the little wooden sloop-of-war stored neatly away in a cabinet. It was still intact. George examined the tiny engine and saw that there were only a few specks of rust. He cleaned the metal with a sanded cloth and oil. Then he demonstrated how the engine worked.

His son was delighted and asked if he might keep it to show his friends. "It's yours, George," Westinghouse replied. "But first I want to take it to the plant."

The next day he demonstrated the rotary engine to several of the company engineers. "See how the jet of steam is piped into the housing to spin the blades?" he told them. "Well, in this case I used it to turn a shaft attached to the ship's paddle wheel. But it seems to me the same principle can be used to rotate a dynamo."

"May I see that, Chief?" an engineer named Keller said eagerly. He took the ship from Westinghouse and examined it carefully.

"What's the matter, Keller?" George asked. "You look surprised."

"I am, Mr. Westinghouse. Why, several weeks ago I happened to read an article in a British engineering journal about an engine invented by an Englishman named Parsons. It operates on this same rotary idea. He calls it the turbine principle."

"That *is* a coincidence," George agreed. "Is Parsons' engine in commercial use?"

"He's developed it to the point of powering a full-sized vessel," the engineer informed him. "The ship is even called the *Turbinia*."

The next morning Keller brought in the engineering journal. George read the article carefully. The turbine was just as the engineer had described it. While it appeared to contain certain technical defects, according to the magazine, the basic principle had proven to be sound.

George lost no time. "I want you to go to England, Keller," he said. "I want you to examine the turbine, and if it has merit I want you to buy it."

In less than two months the engineer returned to America with the design and patent rights to Parsons' engine. Although somewhat crude it had the ability to rotate at amazingly high speeds. Moreover, the turbine was only a fraction of the size of reciprocating engines with the same power output.

George assigned his engineers to improve Parsons' design. Within three years they built small experimental machines that were capable of replacing the old style reciprocators used to power the machine tools in the Westinghouse Air Brake Company. And through additional improvements the power was gradually increased.

The turbine was lighter, more compact, more efficient and less costly than the reciprocator. In addition, it required less fuel, lubrication and attendance, thus cutting down the cost of producing electricity while increasing the current output of generators many times.

By the time the new century arrived, the steam turbine was well on its way to revolutionizing the field of electrical power production throughout the United States and the rest of the world.

16

The Dynamo Is Stilled

THE YEARS GAVE THE IMPRESSION OF SPEEDING BY NOW. YOUNG George would soon be ready for college. Uncertain of his future he asked his father one day what he should do. As an only child he had always been close to his parents, and particularly to his father whom he worshipped. George was aware of his son's deep love and respect for him, and he knew that the youngster would do anything he wished. Deep in his heart his fervent wish had always been that the boy would follow in his footsteps, and he sometimes smiled to himself when he realized that it was only now, when he was over fifty, that he could understand the hopes and dreams his father had for him so many years ago.

Young George had never shown the early signs of inventive genius that George had demonstrated as a boy, but he was bright and alert and had often indicated a keen understanding of mechanical things. In spite of it, George felt it would be wrong to try to force him into a mold of his choosing, as his father had tried to do, so he told his son that the decision must be his alone.

"I have tried to guide you properly and to encourage you to follow your interests wherever they may lead you," he said. "Beyond that, George, it would be wrong of me to shape your life for you. If you still want time to think things over and to explore possibilities—whether a month, a year or more—that's all right. But whatever you finally decide to do, I want you to pour your heart and your mind into it. Your decision will have to last you a long time—for the rest of your life, in fact."

By the time young George was eighteen and ready to enter college, he had made up his mind to become an engineer so that eventually he could work with his father.

More years sped by, and George, silver-haired and distinguished-looking, found it hard to believe he was nearing sixty. He suspected it was this very awareness of the swift passage of time that was the mark of advancing age. Often on a warm spring afternoon he stared wonderingly out of his office window at the lush green miracle of the earth's renewal and felt vague stirrings of regret that for him the beginning was in the past. How he wished he were young George now, just starting out in a world that was on the threshold of a new Golden Age.

It was hard to believe how much life had changed, indeed the world had changed, in the past half-century since he was a boy. In these fifty years man had made more progress in improving his physical lot than in the past thousand years. Many of the diseases that formerly killed had been conquered; communication with the most distant corners of the world could now be accomplished in a matter of a split second; and more products to make life comfortable were available to more people than ever before in history. Who, for example, would have dared to dream fifty years ago that there would be carriages propelled, not by horses but by a gas engine? Or that people would be able to take photographs that gave the illusion of movement when projected on a screen? Or that two young bicycle mechanics named Wilbur and Orville Wright would construct a heavier-than-air machine that could actually fly?

These were magnificent accomplishments—miracles—George thought. And yet he couldn't help wondering whether man hadn't come too far and too fast in that short space of half a century. Man had succeeded in conquering

Nature but he hadn't yet succeeded in harnessing his own wild and obdurate spirit. Perhaps what was needed was time, a breathing spell, to give man a chance to think things over, to learn how to control the marvelous new devices that had been placed at his disposal, to triumph over his own fears and misgivings. Distrust between nations was still the order of the day. Wars were still being fought, and they were bloodier and more destructive than ever. Selfishness and avarice in individuals were still considered unavoidable, if unfortunate, facets of human nature.

George knew, however, that in spite of human shortcomings man would never cease searching and groping into the physical unknown, for as long as human beings existed they would quest and probe, in their thirst to conquer new worlds. This was the basic spirit of mankind, and it would never change without the very nature of man himself changing. No, there was only the dim, optimistic hope that in the decades to come, in young George's lifetime, perhaps, or in the lifespan of young George's children, the unquenchable desire of the human spirit for factual knowledge would translate itself into a search for spiritual knowledge as well. There was the dream that men someday would learn to harness the best instincts of humanity just as they had learned to harness the fruitful earth and the surging waters and the roaring wind.

For himself, George knew he had had a full and satisfying life, and no man could ask for more. He had been blessed with excellent health, an adoring family and a chance to do the work he loved best. For these great gifts he felt humbly grateful. He was fully aware that many men in his position would gladly have retired to enjoy the rewards of past achievement, but for him gratitude seemed to carry with it a burden of debt. Just the very thought of stopping while he still had something to give left him with an uneasy sense of guilt.

So each morning like clockwork he arrived at the plant

in time to greet the first shift and stayed on for the full working day. To his employees his silver white hair and flowing mustache were as familiar and reassuring as the plant buildings in which they earned their livelihood.

Although administrative duties took up most of his time, he devoted an hour or two each day at his drawing board working on some new invention. As a draftsman he was meticulous, so much so that at times his associates argued that his time was much too valuable to waste on routine drafting work. "Why not do a rough sketch and let the draftsmen take over from there?" they suggested.

He shook his head and replied, "It's my method of relaxing. Besides I know of no better way to discover the kinks in a new idea than to try to work it out on the drafting board."

By 1905 George had more than three hundred patents to his credit! In addition to his earlier inventions these included a startling array ranging from gas engines and complicated electrical controls to an improved design for turbine blades. Younger Westinghouse employees were often incredulous upon learning of the monumental accomplishments of the "old man." A youthful engineer once told him admiringly, "Mister Westinghouse, if you had been three men I still would be amazed."

In 1907, just when life seemed to be haloed in a mellow, peaceful glow, the dark clouds of a gathering storm appeared on the horizon. The Westinghouse policy of refusing to join other companies in trusts or combines to fix prices and restrain competition had angered his competitors. True, George's stubborn brand of independence had succeeded in defeating the Edison interests, but it had also created important enemies in high financial circles. The first years of the new century had seen a growing trend toward the formation of powerful trusts in business and industry. Aggressive investment bankers and financial speculators had succeeded in capturing control of many companies through the manipulation of stock and banking funds. Their goal was to increase profits by eliminating competition through mergers.

To the financial barons who now controlled a great segment of American industry, George's refusal to sign agreements to curb free competition constituted a threat. In retaliation they saw to it that he was denied loans from the nation's leading banks, and the Westinghouse companies were forced to turn to other sources to obtain expansion capital. Stock and bond issues were floated and sold to individual stockholders. Or else loans were obtained from the smaller independent banks. In many instances George was forced to use his own funds to tide his companies over difficult periods.

This method of independent financing succeeded largely because of George's personal prestige and reputation for scrupulous honesty. His companies prospered. By 1907, for example, the Westinghouse Electric Company, largest of George's enterprises, was doing more business than it could handle. Moreover, with plans for the manufacture of new products already in the works, prospects for the future seemed brighter than ever before.

At this time the company's outstanding bonds and debts totaled forty-three million dollars. But George was not the least disturbed. He was convinced of the basic strength of the company and felt certain he could renew the loans without difficulty, just as he had always managed to do before.

Then, in October of that year rumors began to circulate that the nation was about to undergo a severe financial crisis. Investors, fearful of losing their money, began to sell heavily on the stock market. Stock values dropped. In a matter of days the panic spread like wildfire throughout the financial world. The banks, eager to protect the savings of their depositors, sharply curtailed credit.

Among the outstanding debts of the Westinghouse Electric Company was a loan of nine million dollars held by

Pittsburgh bankers that had just fallen due. This was not a huge sum compared to the assets of the company, but in the prevailing atmosphere of fear George's request for a renewal of the loan was turned down.

In desperation, he turned to other banks, including the New York banks that had helped him weather the financial crisis of fifteen years before. They, too, rejected his plea.

The companies under the control of the large trusts and combines were protected during the crisis because they had the backing of powerful groups of bankers. The independents, like George's firms, had nobody to turn to. As soon as it appeared that the Westinghouse Electric Company was in deep water the financial speculators and investment bankers gloated. Some tried to hasten the company's ruin by bringing additional pressure to have its loans foreclosed.

For once George found himself helpless. Floundering in a crisis not of his own making, his one thought now was to protect his stockholders and the others who had put their faith in him. He called in his lawyers and instructed them to place the company in receivership.

The courts approved the action. A group of bankers was called in to reorganize the company, and they immediately elected a new board of sixteen directors who appointed as chairman a conservative lawyer named Robert Mather. George remained on as president, and his next move was to submit a reorganization plan to Mather and the others. The proposal took fourteen months to implement, but it proved to be so successful that by the spring of 1909 the Westinghouse Electric Company was solvent again.

George was eager to return at once to the program of research and experimentation that had been the basis for the company's success in the past, but his recommendations were turned down by Chairman Mather who insisted on "conservative, responsible management policies." The quarrel grew to bitter proportions. George, stubborn and independent as always, stood his ground. So did Mather.

The issue was referred to the board of directors. They

upheld their chairman and invited George to take a six-month "vacation." Deeply hurt and disillusioned he decided there was no recourse but to announce his retirement from the company. However, in so doing he agreed to allow it to continue to use his name.

Marguerite tried to console him by pointing out that he still was the president of the Air Brake Company and the other Westinghouse enterprises.

"That's so," George replied. "And I have no intention of resigning myself to a life of inactivity. But I can't help feeling that I carry a good share of the blame for what happened. Perhaps if I had been more conservative and cautious in managing the company—"

"I don't believe a word of that," Marguerite retorted quietly. "I don't think you do, either. After all it was your spirit that founded and built the company, George. The policies you followed were dictated by *your* conscience, no one else's. You did what you felt you must do, honestly and without apology. For that I'm proud and thankful."

George squeezed his wife's hand gratefully and said, "I suppose, Marguerite, that history alone will determine whether I was right or wrong."

At her insistence George agreed to a brief vacation before resuming his busy activities. They spent a week visiting New York City with their son George, who had taken a job as an engineer at the air brake plant after graduating from college, and his young English bride Violet.

When they returned to Pittsburgh Westinghouse plunged right back into his former routine—up at six-thirty in the morning and hard at work at his desk by eight o'clock.

One weekend Marguerite suggested a ride in the family automobile. The car had been presented to George sometime before as a gift from the French Westinghouse Works. He himself distrusted the noisy new contraption that coughed and jerked and snorted clouds of smoke as it rattled along. He preferred "more reliable modes of transportation" such as the railroad or horse and buggy. However, Marguerite was fascinated by the "horseless carriage," so George relented.

As the automobile chugged and bounced its way along a narrow dirt road Marguerite, giggling like a schoolgirl, hung on to her husband for dear life. In the front seat the chauffeur muttered under his breath as he fought to steer clear of the bumps and ruts along the way.

Suddenly the car leaped violently as the front wheels struck an obscure mound. George was thrown out of his seat and his head struck the roof of the vehicle. The chauffeur braked the car to a grinding halt.

"Are you all right, dear?" Marguerite asked anxiously.

"Well, it wasn't fatal," George remarked sourly, as he gingerly fingered his head. "Just a bruise. But I can think of more pleasant ways to spend a Sunday afternoon."

The chauffeur climbed out to examine the car. "There's no damage, sir," he called out as he peered under the chassis. "Nothing broken underneath that I can see."

"That's too bad," George retorted as he continued to explore the tender spot on his forehead. "It would almost be worth a bruise not to have to ride in this instrument of torture again."

As the car started to move once more, George couldn't help grinning. When Marguerite asked him the reason he told her, "The last time I was thrown off a seat while traveling I ended up with an invention—the car replacer. That was almost forty-five years ago. Unfortunately this accident won't be quite as productive."

"Perhaps you'll invent something this time, too," she observed with a smile.

"Not likely," he said. "I have no affection for the horseless carriage. However, I can tell you that if anyone were to come up with an invention to guarantee a comfortable automobile ride, humanity would be in his debt forever."

"Now there's something for you to invent."

George laughed at this preposterous notion.

Nevertheless the following evening out of sheer curiosity he went down to the shed to examine the car. He put on a pair of overalls and crawled under the vehicle, using a small lamp for illumination. It was the first time he had studied the machine closely. What struck him immediately was the crudeness of the suspension system. It consisted simply of long steel strips bound together to serve as springs to support the body. In this respect it was not too different from the springs used on horse-drawn vehicles.

While metal springs might be fine for a slow-paced horse and buggy, he decided, it was entirely inadequate for the jars and jolts of a heavy automobile racing along a bumpy road. But what about compressed air? . . . he mused thoughtfully.

George returned to the house. For the rest of the evening he sat at his desk patiently sketching on a scratch pad. When Marguerite asked him what he was doing he replied, "Meeting the challenge you set for me." Then he explained his project. "What the automobile needs is a device to help the metal springs cushion the shock more effectively. A second set of springs, you might say."

"Then why don't you do just that? Put on additional metal springs."

He laughed. "No, that won't do, dear. No matter how many springs there are or how heavy, the vehicle will still ride roughly. An entirely new principle has to be found."

"Do you have any notions, George?"

"This may surprise you, but I'm of a mind to go back to the medium that made the railroad brake possible—air."

"Air? I don't understand," she said.

"You will, as soon as I finish the design," he promised.

By the next afternoon George had solved the problem with amazing simplicity. He had designed two telescoping cylinders, one of which was to have leather packing and made to slide into the other. To provide an airtight joint he would have oil flow past the packing with the aid of a simple interior pump arrangement.

What he had actually done was to create a "cushion" of compressed air that absorbed shock far more effectively than metal springs. "If this device functions as I think it will, there is no reason why every automobile shouldn't be equipped with it someday," he predicted with his old air of self-confidence. "It's simple, inexpensive and easy to install or replace."

When his mechanics finished constructing the first experimental set of air springs—or "shock absorbers" as they preferred to call them—George had the cylinders installed in the Westinghouse automobile. On a sunny May morning George, Marguerite and their son and his wife set out on a test drive. The chauffeur was instructed to choose the worst road he knew.

As the vehicle clanked noisily along a dusty, unpaved street, striking bumps and holes with regularity, Marguerite stared at her husband in awe. "You've done it, George!" she exclaimed. "Why one would hardly know he was riding in an automobile."

It was true. The ride was so smooth they could hardly feel the jars and jolts. Even the chauffeur grinned and said to his employer, "Your 'shock absorbers' make driving a pleasure, sir. Trying to hold her on an even keel along a road like this was quite a chore before."

"There are tremendous commercial possibilities in these air springs," young George declared enthusiastically.

"You think so, do you?" his father replied.

"I do."

"Then how would you like to go into business with an old man to manufacture these gadgets?"

"Do you really mean that, Father?"

"I do, indeed."

In 1910 the Westinghouse Air Spring Company was organized with the elder Westinghouse as president and his son as vice-president. In a short time production of the revolutionary device was under way. It grew in popularity so quickly that within a few years George's prediction was borne out, and the shock absorber became basic equipment on all automobiles.

In 1913 George and Marguerite spent the summer in
Lenox, Massachusetts. One afternoon George decided to go
fishing on a nearby lake. Although it was August the air
was crisp. When he got to the water's edge he found that
his regular rowboat was not at its mooring. A substitute
had been left in its place. Recalling that one of the dock
employees had said something about the boat being in need
of repairs, he assumed the substitute had been put there for
his use. He climbed into it, but immediately the little craft
began to ship water. In a few seconds George found himself
thoroughly drenched. He climbed out of the sinking boat,
clambered up the steep bank with his clothes dripping and
headed back for the house.

That night he developed chills and coughing. Marguerite
put him to bed. She sent for a physician who ordered rest
and medication. "In addition to taking cold, I think he must
have strained his heart," the doctor told Marguerite. "After
all, he's sixty-seven years old."

The illness proved severe and George had to remain in
bed for many weeks. Afterward, it left him so weakened that
the physician ordered him confined to a wheelchair.

He was incapacitated for months, unable to take more
than a few steps by himself. Marguerite rented a suite of
rooms in New York City where he could have the services
of medical specialists.

On the morning of March 12, 1914, George asked his
nurse to wheel him into the parlor so he could enjoy the
warmth of the sunshine. "I feel even more tired than usual,"
he said. "Perhaps I'll try to nap." The nurse covered him
with a heavy wool blanket and went about her duties.

When Marguerite came into the parlor a few minutes
later her husband's eyes were closed and he seemed to wear
an expression of utter peace and contentment.

"George," she whispered softly. "Are you awake?"

There was no answer.

George Westinghouse was dead at the age of sixty-eight.
A few days later his body was laid to rest in the National

Cemetery at Arlington, Virginia, where America's heroes, military and civilian, are buried. The entire nation mourned.

In the years since his passing, George Westinghouse has been honored as one of history's greatest inventors and as a leading pioneer of the industrial age. The honors have taken many forms. The companies he founded still bear his name, and in 1930, a magnificent memorial was unveiled in Schenley Park, Pittsburgh, paid for by the voluntary contributions of sixty thousand Westinghouse employees. In 1955, he joined other leading figures of American history whose busts stand in the Hall of Fame for Great Americans at New York University.

The spirit of George Westinghouse is perpetuated also in the words others have spoken about him. "He is one of those few men," Nikola Tesla, the electrical genius, once declared, "who conscientiously respect intellectual property, and who acquire their right to use the inventions of others by fair and equitable means."

Samuel Gompers, distinguished labor leader and founder of the American Federation of Labor, said of him: ". . . If all employers of men treated their employees with the same consideration he does, the A. F. of L. would have to go out of existence."

But most of all, the Westinghouse spirit lives on in the hearts of visionaries everywhere who see as life's main purpose the betterment of the human condition for all generations to come.

Bibliography

Beckhard, Arthur J. *Electrical Genius: Nikola Tesla.* New York: Julian Messner, Inc., 1959.

Byrn, Edward W. *The Progress of Invention in the Nineteenth Century.* New York: Munn, 1900.

Clark, T. C. *The American Railway.* New York: Charles Scribner's Sons, 1897.

Cooley, Thomas M. *The American Railway, Its Construction, Development, Management and Appliances.* New York: Charles Scribner's Sons, 1897.

Crane, Frank. *George Westinghouse.* New York: W. H. Wise & Company, 1925.

Faris, John T. *Men Who Conquered.* New York and Chicago: Fleming T. Revell Company, 1922.

Garbedian, H. Gordon. *George Westinghouse: Fabulous Inventor.* New York: Dodd, Mead & Company, 1943.

George Westinghouse, 1846-1914. East Pittsburgh: Westinghouse Electric Company.

George Westinghouse Commemoration: A Forum Presenting the Career and Achievements of George Westinghouse on the 90th Anniversary of His Birth. New York: The American Society of Mechanical Engineers, 1937.

Jaffe, Bernard. *Men of Science in America.* New York: Simon and Schuster, Inc., 1946.

Kaempffert, Waldemar. *A Poular History of American Invention.* New York: Charles Scribner's Sons, 1924.

Kirkland, Edward C. *A History of American Economic Life.* New York: F. S. Crofts and Co., 1934.

Leupp, Francis E. *George Westinghouse: His Life and*

Achievements. Boston: Little, Brown and Company, 1918.

Prout, Henry G. *A Life of George Westinghouse.* New York: Charles Scribner's Sons, 1922.

Taussig, F. W. *Inventors and Money-Makers.* New York: The Macmillan Co., 1930.

Wilson, Mitchell. *American Science and Invention.* New York: Simon and Schuster, Inc., 1954.

Index

185

About the Author

I. E. LEVINE is a native New Yorker. He graduated from DeWitt Clinton High School and enrolled at the City College of New York as a physics major. After working on the college newspaper for two years, he was convinced that he wanted to be a writer and changed his major to English and the social sciences. He received his degree, went to work in the public relations department at City College, and in 1954 was appointed to his present post of Director of Public Relations. He has written many articles for national magazines, is co-author of several adult books and well known for his biographies for young people. He and his family make their home in Kew Gardens Hills, Long Island.